GOD IN MY COFFEE
My Cup Overflows

Dr. Sherry B. Scott, Ph.D.

FOREWORD BY Letitia L. Elliott

Xulon Press

Copyright © 2008 by Dr. Sherry B. Scott, Ph.D.

God In My Coffee
My Cup Overflows
by Dr. Sherry B. Scott, Ph.D.

Printed in the United States of America

ISBN 978-1-60647-499-0

All rights reserved solely by the author. The author guarantees all contents are original and do not infringe upon the legal rights of any other person or work. No part of this book may be reproduced in any form without the permission of the author. The views expressed in this book are not necessarily those of the publisher.

Unless otherwise indicated, Bible quotations are taken from The New International Version Parallel Bible, Copyright © 1985 by Zondervan Corporation, and The King James Version.

www.xulonpress.com

TABLE OF CONTENTS

Dedication vii

Acknowledgements ix

Foreword.. xi

Introduction... xiii

Chapter One: God is…… 21

Chapter Two: God's Healing Love 29

Chapter Three: How To Accept God's Love:
                       A Heart of Repentance.........43

Chapter Four: Growing in God's Love:
                       Are you a Seeker?.................67

Chapter Five:	Set Apart for God's Purpose	85
Chapter Six:	It's Time to Worship	103
Chapter Seven:	Overflowing Blessings of God's Love	119
Chapter Eight:	A Heart of Thanksgiving	129
Chapter Nine:	The Blessing	135
Chapter Ten:	Epilogue: The Gift of Salvation	141

Suggestions for Following Jesus Today 145

Words of Encouragement for Difficult Times 147

References 149

DEDICATION

This book is dedicated to my mother, Elizabeth T. Brown, who taught me how to prayer and live for Jesus. She set an example everyday, while she lived, without forcing religion on her children. Spiritually, she continues to inspire me to follow the leading of the Holy Spirit and let all of the distractions "roll off, like water off a duck's back." Mother, I want to thank you for the life you lived both in spirit and in truth.

This book is also dedicated to you, the reader. May you continue to search for truth and righteousness and find your answers in the Word of God.

GOD BLESS YOU

ACKNOWLEDGEMENTS

I want to acknowledge, first and foremost, my Lord and Savior Jesus Christ. He gently framed and directed my life experiences towards writing this book. I often wondered why He put the desire in my heart to wonder the "how to's" of the Word of God. Now I understand; it's not my will but His will to be done, through His supernatural best.

Thank you to my family for your ongoing love and support. To my husband, David; my sons; Leon, Lance, and Lincoln; my daughter, Loretta; and my daughter-in-law, Marie you are truly gifts from God. A special thanks to my son Lincoln who kept reminding me when I was typing on the computer: "Keep pushing those keys, every time you push down you're stomping on the devil's head."

Special gratitude and appreciation go to Marian R. Hardy, Clayonia C. Dorsey, Loretta A. Scott who patiently assisted with editing and reading the manuscript. Marian thanks for the many hours of reading

God In My Coffee

and re-editing, and most of all thanks for listening to me as I shared ideas and inspirations from the Holy Spirit. Marian, Clay, and Loretta thank you for your words of wisdom and ongoing friendship.

I gratefully acknowledge and sincerely thank Letitia A. Elliot who suggested this great book title and inspired me to keep writing. You have been a wonderful friend and spiritual mentor. I also want to acknowledge the following people, all of who have uniquely contributed to this endeavor. Heartfelt thanks are expressed to my sisters: Lynne Marie, Carolyn, and LaWanda and my brother Robert (Bobby). Thank you for all of your encouragement. I also want to acknowledge my brother Gary C. Brown who has a heart of gold. Keep following Jesus; read the Bible and the "Our Daily Bread." Sincere thanks to my Pastor, D. Wendel Cover and Lois Cover and to all my loving encouragers.

FOREWORD

The day I received the manuscript of this book, the Lord reminded me that precious things are to be shared. This book is undoubtedly the clearest and most direct encouragement in your ability to engage God in a relationship that HE would be most pleased with, even if you are a new babe in Christ. For those of you who read this book out of curiosity, my friend Dr. Sherry Scott, will give you ample opportunities to become acquainted with an Awesome GOD, Friend, and Lover, like you have never known.

The times that you and I are living in now are called the "Last Days." I truly believe that there will not come another generation after this last one (See Matthew 23 – the entire chapter). God, by His Spirit (the Holy Ghost) is drawing, calling, and bringing us closer and closer to Him. He is challenging believers all over the world to come closer to Him. We must know, obey, and be able to hear His voice and fulfill His plan for our lives. This book, is designed to help

God In My Coffee

us – "Get There." Read carefully the instructions you will be given through this wonderful, God inspired, fireside chat along with your beverage and drink all that God will speak in your ear and put in your heart.

I was struck as I read these wonderful God inspired words from the Lord through my sister, friend, and confidant, Dr. Sherry Scott: "The Lord, God wants to constantly pour out His love like cream in our coffee, so that we may experience HIS sweetness." If your relationship with God has been in park, this book will put it in drive again and mobilize the gifts God has put in you to bless the Body of Christ and the world.

Hold on tight. You are going on a wonderful journey that will draw you closer to God, help you in your relationship with others and teach you how to be a great blessing to the Body of Christ.

Letitia L. Elliott
Friend, Psalmist, Teacher

INTRODUCTION

It's time to rest. Relax and take in what the Lord God has to offer you. For every question you have pondered and thought you understood, yet it didn't pan out, have a seat. For every hurt you have experienced and anger that is just under the surface, have a seat and a cup of coffee. I invite you to sit down and have a cup of coffee or tea with me. Let me introduce you to the one I love. Come and meet the one who will take all of your fears, hurts, burdens, and cares. As a friend once said to me "when you have looked all around for a place to sit—come over here and sit with me." Someone is here to answer you, to hold you, cry with you, meditate with you and wait with you. So many of us have tried everything possible to figure out where to go from here—well, have a seat. I know someone you just have to meet.

Do you ever feel like you're spinning in circles or running on a hamster wheel? It's time to step off and have a sit. I want to share with you what has been shared with me. For years my husband would comment, jokingly, Sherry is a "how to" person. All my life I have enjoyed searching and explaining the "how to's" of things. How ironic the Lord gave me the ultimate "How To". So here we go – have a seat, get your cup of coffee or tea, and let's chat about "how to" find and follow Him — the Lord God.

Have you ever been in love? How long did that last—for a few dates and then it was over? Have you ever experienced a one night stand? Well, this book is about how God desires to love you with an everlasting love that will never end. The Lord God desires to spend time with us because *He loves us*. This love – the love that comes from the Father, Son, and Holy Spirit is the First love, and therefore, is the spring from which flows every other form of true love – marital love, mother's love, brotherly love, love of one another, and all genuine love (ICR, 2008). This primary love was expressed through God first when He gave us the gift of His precious son, Jesus who came to share the good news about God's love. When Jesus walked on the earth He was the only man who healed, delivered, and sought to save those who were lost. When Jesus died on the cross for us, He covered us with His blood and made a way for us to walk this life. Jesus said, "I tell you the truth; that it is expedient that I go away for if I go not away, the Comforter" (the Holy Spirit) will not come unto you. But if I depart, I will send Him unto you" (John 16: 7-8). Through the Holy Spirit many believers are now learning to share the gospel throughout the world. I love this promise that even

God In My Coffee

after His death, Jesus sent His Holy Spirit who lives within us. He will never ever leave us or forsake us. The Holy Spirit teaches us how to follow Jesus' example. All this was done for each and every one of us because of God's eternal and unconditional love. Oh, so much love He continuously lathers on us.

We all like gifts and our Heavenly Father offers many gifts to us. After He gave the gift of His most precious son, Jesus, God gave to us the gift of His Holy Spirit. All we have to do is reach out and receive this wonderful gift that Jesus gave us after His resurrection and ascension into heaven.

Scripture Promise: James 1:17

Every good gift and every perfect gift is from above, and comes down from the Father of Lights, with whom there is no variableness, neither shadow of turning.

The gift of the Holy Spirit enlightens us about the word and how to apply it a little more each day. Learning how to follow Jesus comes by communing or spending time with Him as we read His word (the Bible). Just as God spent time with Adam in the cool of each day He still longs to spend time with His children each day. In my life, the cool (best time) of each day is early in the morning, when I pray and meditate while having a cup of coffee. Most days I sit at my kitchen table, look out the window, and ponder the word and wonder of God. When I meet with Him daily I begin to hear His voice. When I let go of trying to reason or understand why things are happening then little by little I begin to understand the Lord's way better. So, it's time to get your favorite mug, whether you like tea or coffee, and let's fill it up. As we commune with the Lord through the power of His Holy Spirit then He will fill our spiritual cup (heart) so much that it overflows.

Each day, stop, have a cup of coffee, rest and meditate on the Word of God. Don't be in a hurry because God's not in a hurry. Matter of fact, as you sit right now God is with you because He is always there. When a cup of coffee is brewing, we wait for it. It tastes so much better than microwave or instant coffee. God desires to brew us rather than microwaving us with quick unprepared results. The Lord God even tells us in the Psalms, "Oh, taste and see that the Lord is good." You can't experience the sweet taste of the Lord without spending time with His Son Christ Jesus through the power of the Holy Spirit. The Lord God is good to the last drop.

This book is written as a source of encouragement and practical application of how to receive and walk with the Lord. The Lord God draws us to Himself through unconditional love. God is love. It is God's goodness and constant love that is being poured into us and developing in us a desire to please Him and obey His voice. We love God because He first loved us. Jesus is real and alive and He desires to share Himself with us. He will not force himself on us. God pursues us through His Holy Spirit and draws us to Himself with a sweet abiding love. But,

God In My Coffee

we have to answer the knock on the door of our heart and let Him in. Try Him you might like Him!

We dwell on and seek out things that are important to us. If you observe yourself and your behavior patterns in one day you will notice what you dwell on and how you spend time through the day, on people or things that are important to you. One of the best examples I can describe is how I sought, studied, and meditated on something that was very important to me – when I was working on my doctorate degree. In order to complete my Ph.D., I had to prepare a large manuscript which required many hours of research and dedication. It took months and years to finish the degree. The initial process required seeking out information about a certain topic – in my case homelessness. I studied, meditated, and immersed myself into the topic. Some scholars say you practically become wedded to the topic area. When we want to fully understand someone or something that we are passionate about, we give it our full attention, time, and act on it. This same process occurs in areas of our lives in which we are truly interested. Sometimes we seek out and desire material things with the same vigor, for example, new technologies, shopping, seeking information or things on the internet.

Another example of how God pursuing us is like a wedding engagement. In the engagement process we begin building a close relationship with someone by spending time with them. This is usually a period of courtship and pursuit. As we seek Jesus through the Bible, which is our blue print on how to know and follow Jesus, we find that he has already been pursuing us to give *Everlasting Love*.

This book reveals how we can follow the Lord God in today's confusing and warring society. The more difficult the times are, the more God desires to reveal, draw, and equip His children for victorious living. We just have to ask His advice – believing it is true. Today, God longs to lead us through this process together empowered by the Holy Spirit. Following Jesus is truly a journey of surrendering our old ways of doing things and drawing nearer to God and following His ways (Deut 5:22). Learning to walk in love is a lifelong process that becomes better and more consuming daily for those who choose to follow Jesus. In the Book of John, chapter ten, verse four Jesus said "My sheep know my voice." This is still true. If you listen with your heart you can still hear Him. Let's explore this exciting journey together not only to read about it but to act on the promises and blessings of God's love. Therefore, after each chapter the reader is invited to participate and answer a spiritual growth activity or "Triumphant Strategies" Worksheet.

Before we read, let's pray, "Holy Spirit enlighten us about the word of God and how to apply it more and more each day." The more we know Him and seek Him, the more we realize how wonderful He is. Just as in any other healthy relationship we fall more and more in love. This love leads to a desire to be like Him and follow Him, which then leads to an overflowing abiding relationship. He fills our spiritual cup with an overflow of His unconditional love that spills over and flows out into loving others, even our enemies. This overflowing love reaches out to others as He teaches us His unconditional love (Matthew 22:37 – 38). Hence, the book **"God in My Coffee: My Cup Overflows."**

CHAPTER ONE:

GOD IS……

I AM the Alpha and Omega, the First and the Last

Revelation 1: 11

The way we view God directly impacts how we believe, trust, and worship Him. The question is: **Who is God? How do you see God in your life?** God is Love. God is good and His mercy endures forever. Another name for God is Jehovah. There are many names that describe the characteristics of Jehovah. Each name describes one facet of Him – about who He is in our lives. El Elyon is seeing God as High and Lifted up, Almighty God, creator of the heavens and earth. This name is the name we learned about as children in Sunday school. We believe that God Almighty is omnipotent (all powerful), omnipresent (all seeing and everywhere), and omniscience (all knowing). Well, God is still Almighty. Matter of

God In My Coffee

fact, another name, El Shaddai, reminds us that He is all powerful and all sufficient. The Lord God has not changed. He is the same today, tomorrow, and yesterday. Only our belief has changed. Since God our Father is all sufficient, all powerful, and all knowing then we believe He knows our needs and wants (Jehovah Jireh). He knows them before we ask for help. The question is do we believe this enough to act on it? Will we pray and believe that He sees and will provide for our needs? The answer is, yes. Trust God enough to believe that He knows the timing of when it will happen and how. Our job is to believe that God is able (El Shaddai), trust that He has it all under His control (El Elyon), and wait patiently for Him (El Rohi). Meanwhile, keep moving forward in what He told you to do at home, work, and during interactions with others in your life. Our relationship with God is not stagnant but dynamic and ever increasing in intimacy and faith.

For each of us today, we have to come to terms with who God really is. He is All- Sufficient, El Shaddai. Since He is All-sufficient, we can let go of our own need to be self-sufficient and believe that Almighty God is in control and able to take care of all of our needs. The real question is: Do we believe God and do we want to get to know Him intimately? It's our choice.

God places special people all around us who are loving and helpful. These people are usually good listeners and encouragers. They have godly influences that direct us back to Almighty God. God has been there all the time but very often He may use

God In My Coffee

people or circumstances to draw us back to Him. Jot down a few names of the people who have been helpful to you over the years and thank God for them. If you can't think of a name then go to a bible-based, teaching church and join a bible study or Sunday school class.

I remember a few years ago I started a new job in a slightly unsafe neighborhood and one day while walking alone on the main street. I said to myself, "I'm all alone right now. No one who is familiar to me really knows where I am." Right at that moment I looked up and a very special friend and colleague was walking towards me and called my name, "Sherry." Immediately, I felt safe and knew that from that time onward I didn't need to fear because God would always be with me – spiritually – and physically, sending me people who cared.

Now it's time to give back by supporting others who may have experienced hurt, fear, pain, and anger and lost their way. I will be real and let you know I have experienced my own pains, but I have chosen to follow God's way through His Son Jesus Christ in the power of His Spirit in order to deal with it. I have given my fears and hurts to the Lord and trust Him rather than try to lean on my old way of dealing with it. He has replaced my fears with joy. Now I acknowledge God's greatness and sufficiency and believe that He directs my path in painful times with His beautiful love, peace, and joy surrounding me as I go through (Proverbs 3: 5-6). If you have tried to deal with pain, hurt, and anger on your own and it has not really worked, then can I suggest we try something else? I know it sounds like a cliché; but I firmly believe that Jesus is the answer. He will heal, deliver, encourage, and carry your burdens as He does for me. And He can do it while we sip our coffee or tea together. He desires to fill our mug with His everlasting waters of refreshing springs. His Spirit will overflow us with love and over time He enables us to help others that He brings into our path. The Lord God truly is our Shepherd, Jehovah Rohi. He knows what you really want. The first things He wants to do for you is, love you and restore you, and then give you a new direction into His path of righteousness. So fill up and let's experience God as All-sufficient, All-powerful, All-knowing, and Almighty – our Good Shepherd who cares for us, His sheep.

In the Psalms King David views God from a very high perspective. He knew God was El Elyon, creator of the heavens and earth. He declares God's glory and His wonders. David gives God majesty, honor, and praise. He also describes God as, All-sufficient, All-Powerful, All-knowing so that He will judge the people righteously. In Psalm 23 the Lord God reveals Himself as, our Shepherd. He draws us with a loving rod and causes us to be confident with leadership. He wants a deep intimate relationship with us to restore our soul. No one can separate us from the love of God when we have intimacy with Christ. As the Lord our Shepherd teaches us how to trust Him more He begins to leads us in the path of righteousness. This psalm gives us direction on "how to" worship and give God glory and honor. In addition, the Lord reminds us that when going through hard times, ie

God In My Coffee

walking through the valley of death, He promises that He will be with us and therefore we do not have to fear. Not only is God with us through the power and presence of His Spirit, He comforts us with His rod and staff. Psalm 23 tells us step by step about another facet of God's character that He is Jehovah Rohi and that He wants to restore, comfort, anoint, and bless us. The psalm is very short and most of us know it by heart. However, let's go back one more time and ask God for spiritual understanding as we re-read it. Allow the Lord to show us Psalm 23 in a fresh and new way and to experience how He wants to take care of us in quiet and difficult times. Make this word confession with me:

Scripture Promise: Psalm 23

The Lord is my Shepherd I shall not be in want
He makes me to lie down in green pastures
He leads me beside still waters; He restores my soul
He leads me in the path of righteousness for His name's sake
Even though I walk through the valley of the shadow of death
I will fear no evil; for You are with me,
Your rod and staff comfort me;
Yu prepare a table before me in the presence of my enemies
You anoint my head with oil; my cup overflows.

God In My Coffee

> Surely goodness and mercy shall follow me all of the days of my life.
> And I will dwell in the house of the Lord, Forever.

Daily prayer, reading, and meditation in the Psalms are great ways to learn how to worship the Lord God and be spiritually strengthened at the same time. The Psalms also teach that true worship can be sacrificial, because at times we may not want to worship. But, as we worship the Lord God anyway He gives us His presence and fullness of joy (Psalm 16:11).

Scripture Promise: Psalm 34:1

> I will bless the Lord at all times
> His praise shall continually be in my mouth

What we believe determines how we relate to God. Is He wonderful and powerful to us? We must choose to believe that God is faithful and true to His name. If we just believe in these attributes about God we begin to experience His amazing, awesome, magnificent love. God is Holy and He wants us to know Him more by receiving His everlasting love.

A few of the names that characterize our Father, Jehovah God are:

1. El Elyon: God Most High, Creator and Possessor of Heaven and Earth

2. El Shaddai: God All-Powerful and All-Sufficient
3. Jehovah Jireh: The Lord Who Sees and Who Provides
4. Jehovah Rohi: The Lord is my Shepherd
5. Jehovah Raphe: Our Healer
6. Jehovah Shammah: The Lord God is There
7. Emmanuel: God is with us
8. Jehovah Shalom: God our Peace
9. Jehovah Nissi: God our Banner
10. Jehovah Tsedkineu: The Lord our Righteousness

CHAPTER TWO:

GOD'S HEALING LOVE

*The Lord says, "I love you
with an everlasting love"*

Jeremiah 31:3

There is a beautiful verse in the Book of Jeremiah where the Lord says, "I love you with an everlasting love." This type of love is deeper and richer than the temporary love that the world offers. Just like cream added to our cup of coffee to smooth out the flavor, The Lord God constantly wants to pour out His love like cream in our lives to let us experience His sweetness. Almighty God, as our heavenly Father, desires to add His gladness to us as we accept His unconditional love to our lives. When we receive God's free gift of love into our lives we begin "tasting" or experiencing the goodness of God

God In My Coffee

from a His new perspective. There is nothing that God's love can't heal!

<u>Scripture Promise: Proverbs 16: 24</u>

Pleasant words are as an honeycomb sweet to the soul, and health to the bones.

The Lord God constantly reminds us that He is Love. I know this sounds simple yet it is so profound. Almighty God is the same yesterday, today, and forever. What He has been offering to us since the beginning of time is Love, which is His very self. His love has never changed because it is the very essence of who He is. Since we are made in God's image, it is His love in us that draws *ALL* mankind. He created us for and to be, Love, as He is. In each one of us is a deep desire for love. When you peel back all the layers of who we are as individuals, there is a fundamental desire for love. That desire comes from God – He created us this way. We may mask the need for love with many different behaviors but when we reflect on our needs and desires we realize our internal need for genuine love. Sometimes, these thoughts are painful because of past hurts.

Well, there's good news, God wants you to have His love and to experience His completeness right now. Sit quietly, take a sip of coffee and let the Lord God fill your spiritual cup with His very essence, Love. Close your eyes right now and ask your Heavenly Father, "Help me Lord to receive your genuine unconditional love right now, in the name

God In My Coffee

of Jesus Christ. Be still, listen, and wait because He wants you to have it right now. I believe this and intercede for you right now, so receive His love. Pause and close you eyes and listen, Amen. Now is your time to receive God's Everlasting Love. His love will never leave us but will abide forever. This love is not based on feeling, that's the world's way. God's love is based on faith. Believe that you have received His genuine love and no one can ever remove His love from you. It is yours forever.

The beauty about God's love and having a personal relationship with Jesus Christ as our Lord and Savior is that He accepts us just the way we are. Because God is love He wants us to receive His love. Sometimes because of our past failures our cup may be so full that we can't believe that anyone could love us. Well it's true and I am a living witness. I tried to hide from God's love, but He saw me, loved me and softly drew me to himself. His love had been there all the time and it is still there today. We need to only believe and receive His love unconditionally. The Lord who created us knows all about us already. He sees us through eyes of love. He wants us to come to Him just the way we are and bring all the old stuff and baggage. As we bring all of our stuff He gently gets rid of our old baggage and builds a intimate relationship with us. He then begins the process of cleaning and restoring us back to Him.

I want to share how God poured His love on me and freed me from the baggage I was carrying. An example of something in my baggage was, my believing that I was not lovable. I had a happy child-

God In My Coffee

hood with both of my parents but while playing with friends and family members I did not understand or feel love. Somehow I knew I was loved but it never seemed to be enough. I started to sense God tugging at my heart almost saying, "try me." This was definitely taking me out of my comfort zone, (what little so called comfort I had). When it came to expressing love, for example, through hugging, I would withdraw. Matter of fact, as an adult the joke became at work, "Sherry doesn't hug." Hugging my husband was easy because after several years of dating and believing he really loved me I got use to his hugs. However, I still did not love myself because I did not understand love. So, I would pull back when it came to other platonic relationships. Not realizing it, the Lord was dealing with me in this area. He was slowly putting people is my life who would give me big "bear type" hugs. After awhile I started to like this. A very good friend of mine recently got married to a wonderful man. When my husband and I would go out with this couple, the husband would greet me with a friendly "bear hugs." Once, after a church service this same friend gave me one of those hugs. Without realizing, I pulled away, turned, and started to cry. It was a cleansing cry from deep inside. I felt that God was freeing me from old baggage. I never felt this before, I knew the Lord was cleansing me by using my friend's husband's friendly "big bear hug" to almost squeeze out the stuff or baggage in my life. I felt God's love in that hug. The next day I called my friend and told her how the Lord used her husband's friendly hug to heal and restore God love back into

God In My Coffee

my life. I had been holding back from receiving His love until God used my friends' husband to help me realize that it was okay to accept love. It's amazing to watch God move in your life because He knows the best timing for healing. In order for me to receive God's love I had to clean out my spiritual cup and let go of old baggage. Then I could allow God to fill my cup with His love. I had to feel safe in His love and believe that He cared for me. Now, I want you to experience His love as well.

The Lord God loves us with "no strings" attached. His very nature is love, therefore, love is what He freely gives. It's our choice to believe and accept His love. He personally wants to teach us how to follow His way of love and goodness. When we believe and confess Jesus as our personal Lord and Savior then God's Spirit, the Holy Spirit, cleans us and prepares us for the day of redemption. Because God lives within us He lovingly reveals His goodness. During this process He also restores us back to Himself. He gently re-directs us in the path of His righteousness. He begins to reveal His love in our lives as the Lord, our Shepherd. I love the verse in Psalm 23 that says "He restores our souls, and leads us in the path of righteousness." The Lord's everlasting love will abide with us forever.

Past experiences in our lives might include love, hurts, pains, adversity, etc. God wants us to come to Him and bring all these experiences. I know this because I've experienced this personally. He is drawing all people back to Him because we were made in His image. He desires to heal our brokenness and reveal His loving presence to us in a very personal way. It is through being broken that God's glorious light can come forth as we do His will. He begins to show us the right way to go, prompting us to follow Him. He knows everything we have been through – whether good or bad. He is our sweet Heavenly Father wooing us back to Him. As we begin to believe that God is good and He really cares for us then we can let go of our burdens and cast them on Him (I Peter 5:7). The more we believe and trust that the Lord loves us the more we begin to see Him as wonderful and beautiful. He shows us compassion and forgiveness (towards ourselves and others). The Lord removes our old baggage and replaces it with Himself—His love, tender mercies, and lovingkindness. When you experience this kind of love you will never want to go back to the old ways. We are hemmed in by His love. We cannot get away from His love nor do we desire to do so because God is the very essence of Love. When we believe this by faith then we begin to see the manifestation of His grace, love, and mercy towards us, and we want more. God desires for us to believe Him and receive His love. In Psalm Chapter 139 the psalmist reminds us that the Lord has hemmed us in – behind and before us and He has laid His hand upon us – surrounding us with His love. Knowing that God is with us and will never leave, sustains us while experiencing life and walking in newness of life because greater is He who is in us then he that is in the world (I John 4:4).

Over the years I believe the Lord has been trying to show me that His love for me is pure and

God In My Coffee

personal—different from what I had experienced in my childhood. He wanted me to receive the deep and rich love that was in store for me. He wanted the cup of my being to be filled with more of Him to the point of overflow. In my spirit I felt He was doing a new thing and that old things and ways would pass away (2 Corinthians. 4:18). God was removing old stuff from my cup and putting in His love as I had never experienced before. In the past, as I ponder about difficult times I felt like I was reaching out for other significant people to fill a gap in my life. But early one morning during a quiet time of meditation the Lord spoke quietly to my spirit and said, "Sherry, that kind of love only comes from me." I opened my eyes as if to say "what". I knew what the Lord had said. It was as if He said, Let me love you. Let me give you such a deep, full, and rich love that only comes from me. This kind of love no person can give. When you experience this love you feel complete. In return, the Lord wants us to love Him back. Now, it is my desire to love the Lord God with all of my heart, soul, and mind, and strength (Matthew 22: 37). Now, I am beginning to understand what the psalmist meant when he wrote, "Lord there is no one that I desire besides you." (Ps 73:14).

It is this love that the Lord God desires to fill you with. He has always loved us. He draws us to Himself, and fills us up to the brim with Him. The beauty of this love is, as you fall more and more in love with the Lord, He loves you back, and then the Holy Spirit teaches us how to love those close to us and not to be dependent on love from others. The Lord desires that

God In My Coffee

we depend on Him for love. Sometimes it's helpful to ponder and question ourselves about love and what we believe. Be honest with your answers. Remember God is a big God and He said come just as you are:

> **Do we believe that God really loves us?**
>
> **Do you think at times God doesn't love you? When?**

God is a great and mighty God and He can handle our questions. Matter of fact, asking importance questions let's Him know that we are serious and we desire to get to know Him more. As we seek Him day by day He fills our cup with more of Him and teaches us how to love ourselves and love others. Our love for those around us is not based on whether or not they love us. It comes from the Lord God. God's love is rich with compassion for others. Through His Spirit, we love and compassion for others and reach out to others in need. Loving others even when love is not given is return, demonstrates sacrificial love for one another. This love is not based on a law but on a desire to please your heavenly Father and maintain intimate fellowship with Him. In essence, the

God In My Coffee

Holy Spirit teaches you how to love others who may be our enemy.

If you believe that God truly is good and His mercy endures forever, then He wants you to share His mercy and love with others. You don't have to worry about figuring out how to always have mercy or love, because the Holy Spirit will teach us His love and mercy. The Holy Spirit lives within us. If we draw near to Him, He will draw near to us, and teach us wondrous things, such as how to love one another. We can not do this on our own strength only by the love of Christ Jesus. Matter of fact, when God looks at His children who are hid in Christ, He sees us through the filter of Jesus and the Holy Spirit.

The world does not teach nor does it understand this type of unconditional love. Matter of fact, the world's love always has strings attached to it. If you do this for me, I will love you. Now that we know God's wonderful love for us, we want ours sons and daughters and everyone else to know and seek God first. No man or women is able to give such love unless it comes from the Lord God Himself. Take the time to develop an intimate love relationship with the Lord God. Spend time with the Lord, seek Him out. God actually loved you first. He will take care of you. Our sufficiency and sustenance comes from God and God alone, through His Holy Spirit. When we realize just how much the Lord loves us – that He gave His only son to die for us (John 3:16) we begin to realize the depth of His love.

Imagine that the Lord as at the door of your heart waiting patiently on the other side. The only door-

God In My Coffee

knob is on your side. You have to open up the door on your side. You have to let Him in. He desires to have a loving intimate relationship with each one of us. This relationship is personal and one on one. The scripture says "love the Lord God with all of your heart, soul, mind, and strength" (Matthew 22:37). The more we love Him the more intimate the relationship. He does not want us dependent on man for love. He wants us to open the door to the Lover of our soul, our first love. This love is rich, deep, full, and abundant. You can only first experience it with the Lord. Experiencing God's love causes us to spiritually decrease and He to increases. He begins to take over in your life and manifest His love through you. When you get a touch of His love, you immediately want to give this love to others, which is the second half of the verse – "to love your neighbor as yourself" (Matthew 22: 37). For years I had been praying that the Lord would increase love, intimacy, and communication in marriages. The Lord recently placed on my heart don't seek to enhance relationships, until you seek love, intimacy, and communication with the Lord God first and an natural outcome will be the increase of your love for others – the first other being those closest to you – spouse, family, children, or friends.

Unfortunately, many believers have forgotten their first love. In Chapter three of the book of Revelations the Lord reminds us to come back to our first love (Revelations 3: 1 – 6). Just as God loves and communes with us with a heart of compassion, mercy, and lovingkindness, He is also a jealous God. He does

God In My Coffee

not want us to put any gods before Him. It's through His love that we live, move and have our being. He created is for His glory. When we reject Him it as if we're saying; I know you love me and created me heavenly Father but I choose not to acknowledge you and give my love to another – that hurts. The Lord longs for us to come back to Him and acknowledge His goodness. Seeking things and stuff to cope with past hurts, wants, and needs cannot totally satisfy. We need to seek God's love. He mends, heals, restores, and renews. There is no other place to receive total satisfaction except through Jesus. Oh come and taste and see that the Lord truly is good. Blessed is the man (or woman) who trusts in God (Psalm 37:8). Only the Lord God can satisfy you every desire. When we are hurting the enemy tries to rob our joy through discouragement and he wants us to doubt God, even to doubt His very existence. These feelings are from Satan because as we said earlier God encourages and lifts us up, Satan discourages. Discouragement is not of God. This is the same thing Satan did to Adam and Eve in the Garden of Eden.

Since the Lord created us and made us relationship oriented eventually everyone has to decide who they will seek and follow. The Lord made us for His glory, praise, and worship. This is His prerogative because he created the heavens and earth and created us (El Elyon) and began communing with Adam and Eve in the cool of each day until they chose to sin and disobey. The rest of man's purpose and existence on the earth has been to bring us back to an intimate relationship with our Heavenly Father, through

God In My Coffee

accepting Jesus Christ as our Lord and Savior and being empowered by God's Holy Spirit. He created us for Him and continually expresses a deep abiding unconditional love for us that will never go away. The enemy has been trying to keep us from God so that we would perish with him in hell. Each person has to choose whom they will seek and follow.

In essence, Jesus fulfilled The Father's plan and purpose by choosing to die for our sins, sending His Spirit to live in each of us, and making a way for us to do our heavenly Father's will. God gave us His only son, Jesus Christ, who demonstrated the ultimate act of love by willingly giving His life for us – suffering and dying on the cross. After Jesus' death and resurrection He sent the Holy Spirit as our Comforter, to live within us. Jesus also promised that He would come back again for those who choose to believe and follow His way. It is the Holy Spirit who prepares and leads us in the path of righteousness for His name sake.

As we grow in God's love we are becoming more spiritually mature. Through the Holy Spirit we learn to seek God through prayer, praise, and meditation on the word of God. Each person is responsible for their own relationship with the Lord. The Lord actually says "learn of me" in Matthew 11: 37. He teaches us how to love even through times of adversity. During the hard times in my life I realize now that God was with me and He was using those experiences to strengthen me. If I had not gone through those things as I did I would have never come out of what felt like a false "comfort zone." I came out kicking and

God In My Coffee

screaming, but thank God He brought me out. With this kind of love, you are set free. You don't want the world's cheap, counterfeit love. God desires that we are all set free in His love. Whom the Lord has set free is free indeed (John 8:36).

I share this testimony to help someone else. It does not matter what your age is, if you have not experienced an ongoing love relationship with the Lord God, for His son Jesus, through the Holy Spirit, now is the time to fall in love and be set free. Come and drink from His cup and take some time right now to be still and ask the Lord for His love. The Lord desires to be our portion and recreate us as relational being. The love relationship comes as you spend time with the Lord.

As we experience the Lord's love He will transform us to be more like Him. Our love for God is also manifest in our desiring to keep His commandments. His first commandments came to His servant Moses. In the Old Testament, Book of Deuteronomy Chapter 30 is: "Oh Israel, The Lord our God is one Lord, Love the Lord your God with all of your heart, all of your soul, and all of your might. And these words I command thee this day, shall be in thine heart." This same command is also given in the New Testament, Matthew Chapter 22: 37. "Love the Lord your God with all of your heart, soul, and mind and the second is like the first to love your neighbor as yourself." The more time you spend with God the more this command becomes our desire.

As our love grows for the Lord God and His Son Jesus Christ our entire being (body, mind, and soul)

God In My Coffee

wants to obey, serve, submit, and surrender ourselves to Him. Receiving God's love and loving Him in return is essential for mature spiritual relationships empowered by the Holy Spirit. As we obey and love God He teaches us how to walk and speak the truth in love. King David in the Old Testament also demonstrated a pure love for God. He was called a "man after God's own heart". His love was so rich and full for the Lord that the Lord God used David's lineage for the Son of God. In the gospels, Matthew, Mark, Luke, and John, Jesus demonstrated by example how we are to love and obey.

In Romans 8:28 that God says: "And we know that all things work together for good to them that **love** God, to them who are called according to His purpose." As we walk in our calling and purpose we realize the things we go through work out for good for those who love the Lord. The reason it works out is because God has our best interest at heart and He can see the beginning from the end. The Lord God loves us so much that He desires to remove past hurt, pain, brokenness and areas of unforgiveness. Through the power of His Spirit He gently brings us to the place of confession and repentance.

CHAPTER THREE:

HOW TO ACCEPT GOD'S LOVE: A HEART OF REPENTANCE

For Whom the Lord Loves He Corrects

Proverb 3:12

The more time we spend with God, reflecting on how wonderful he is the more we realize how sinful we are. It is the Holy Spirit who brings us to an awareness of sin. He teaches us how to confess and repent as we grow and believe God. The Lord wants to remove our sins and pains. It's up to us to believe that God will still love us when we give Him our hurts and pains. God's word says, "now our darkness has past, because God's true light shines in us (I John 2:8)." A scripture promise that we can hold on to and believe that we are forgiven is:

Scripture Promise: (Psalm 103: 11-12)

For as the heaven is high and above the earth; so great is His Love (mercy) towards them that fear (reverence) Him.

As far as the east is from the west, so far has He removed our transgressions (sins) from us (and He remembers them no more).

During prayer and meditation God begins to reveal facets of Himself to us. We see Him as Holy, Mighty, Most High God, Creator of heaven and earth, and All Powerful. One thing the Lord impressed on my heart recently was that God is All Sufficient and is fully in control of all things. He sees and knows all things – therefore we can let go of our sense of self sufficiency. Self-sufficiency means you think you can handle the situation and you try to work it out. When we do this, we are telling God I don't trust you in this particular situation and I don't need your help – I'll handle it. Well, God will not intervene during times of our self-sufficiency until we say, "Lord help me." Then He reminds us that He was there all the time. When He does help us through difficulties and things get better then sometimes we forget His help and go back to our self-sufficiency and might even take the credit. Developing a heart of repentance is a daily process of turning from our self-sufficiency to trusting in God who is All-sufficiency. His grace is sufficient to bring us through hardships.

When one of my sons turned thirteen years old he informed me that he no longer would be going to

God In My Coffee

the children's service because he is now a teenager. Hearing this, the Lord impressed on me that it's the children who are pure in heart. During my prayer time the Lord provided spiritual understanding regarding how the pure in heart. They are those who are lowly, contrite or have a humble heart. Humility is having a childlike faith that believes and depends on God – believing that God is able to do what He said He will do. When people including children, begin to move towards a sense of independence, they try to become more self reliant and self-sufficient. The person begins to depend on his or her own abilities. The more the person experience successes the more they believe they are personally doing it and forget that their capabilities, skills, talents, and gifts come from the Lord God. People begin to doubt God is even doing anything. This is when the enemy creeps in with pride so that we doubt the goodness of God. We forget the greatness of the Creator who created and gifted each person to be creative "in Him" and not in his own capabilities. There is a tendency to see things from our perspective and not view it from God's greatness. Our focus has moved away from God's awesomeness. Therefore, as parents it's our job to help our children to see God as great and to keep a high view of a Him.

A humble and contrite heart (or pure heart) allows us to continue to see things from God's perspective. This is why Jesus said in Matthew Chapter 18 1-5, "except you be converted and become as little children, you shall not enter the kingdom of heaven. Whosoever shall humble himself as this little child,

God In My Coffee

the same is greatest in the kingdom of heaven." A child who learns about Jesus early through reciting wonderful verses is beginning to realize the greatness of God. As children get older, there is a tendency for them to lose some of that innocent dependency on God. This is the time when we choose who we will serve, ourselves or Him (the age of accountability). Now, we have to decide if we will accept Christ and continue believing God with a child like faith and a humble and contrite heart.

When we choose to accept and depend on God then we develop a pure heart and begin to see God from a new perspective – as All Sufficient (El Shaddai) great and awesome God. Therefore we can now trust God to lead and guide our lives. It's almost like a spiritual life cycle. Ultimately, with spiritual growth we are re-learning with a child-like faith "how to" become dependent on Jesus as our personal Lord and Savior and "how to" follow Jesus. As we develop a child-like faith we realize and believe that God is who He says He is: the Great I AM. The Holy Spirit cleanses and purifies us. He teaches us to see that God is great and majestic. We develop a high perspective on God we desire to serve Him, and to seek His call and purpose for our lives, and follow His agenda.

Spiritual Life Cycle

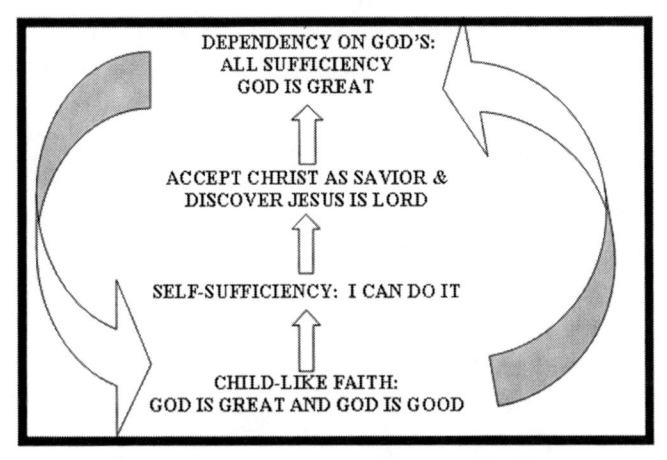

```
         DEPENDENCY ON GOD'S:
           ALL SUFFICIENCY
             GOD IS GREAT
                  ⇧
       ACCEPT CHRIST AS SAVIOR &
        DISCOVER JESUS IS LORD
                  ⇧
       SELF-SUFFICIENCY: I CAN DO IT
                  ⇧
           CHILD-LIKE FAITH:
     GOD IS GREAT AND GOD IS GOOD
```

© 2008 Developed by Sherry B. Scott

As we trust God and believe that He really loves us, then His Holy Spirit begins to prompt us towards an attitude of forgiveness and repentance. It is the Holy Spirit that brings us to this place, not us. On our own, we do not naturally seek forgiveness and repentance because we don't think we have done anything wrong most of the time. In our minds it is usually someone else's fault, not ours. However, God in His infinite love still draws us to Himself.

The Lord desires that we draw near to Him, just the way we are. Then the Holy Spirit will start the process of cleaning us up (James 4:7-9). The cleaning process starts with submission. James 4:7 tells us to submit ourselves to the Lord, resist the devil (our old ways) and he will flee. The next verse says to draw near to the Lord and He will draw nearer to us. We

God In My Coffee

want to be clean so that we can receive His blessings. It's like cleaning out our coffee cups so He can pour and reveal Himself to you. The more we submit and confess the more we recognize His love and presence. One of the sweetest prayers of confession, forgiveness, and repentance that most of us have known for many years is the Lord's Prayer:

Scripture Promise: Matthew 6: 6-9

Our Father who art in heaven hallowed be thy name
Thy kingdom come, thy will be done on earth as it is in heaven
Give us this day our daily bread
Forgive us our debts as we forgive our debtors
Lead us not into temptation, but deliver us from evil
For thine is the kingdom, and the power, and the glory, forever. Amen.

An attitude of repentance should be common practice while we live on this earth because we live in a sin filled world. People don't feel comfortable talking about repentance but without it we can not draw close to our Heavenly Father (spiritually) into the Holy of Holies. We must come clean. We should not think so highly of ourselves that we do not sin. Yes, we do.

The first step towards a heart of repentance is confessing our sins to Jesus. Realizing we have sinned leads us acknowledging our need for a Savior and His forgiveness (Roman 10: 9-10). It is with the confession of our mouths that we are saved and forgiven of our sins. The amazing aspect about confession is once we confess our sins the enemy (Satan) no longer has a hold on us in that particular area. The enemy wants us to dwell on our sins and develop bitterness, anger and unforgiveness. King David understood the power of confession and forgiveness. In Psalm 32 He teaches us how to confess our sins and receive God's forgiveness and blessings. Let's turn together to Psalms Chapter 32 and read rich truths of how to the Lord desires to forgive us. Take a sip of your coffee and meditate on the Holy Word that you are about to read, as follows:

Scripture Promise: Psalm 32: 1- 5

Blessed is he (or she) whose transgression (sin) is forgiven,
Whose sin is covered.
Blessed is the man unto who the Lord imputes not iniquity, and Whose spirit there is no guile.
When I was silent, my bones waxed old through my roaring all the day long. For day and night thy hand was heavy upon me: my moisture is turned into the drought of summer. (Selah) {pause, think about this}
Then I acknowledged my sin unto thee, and mine iniquity have I not hid.

> **I said I will confess my transgressions unto the Lord; and thou forgave the iniquities of my sin.** (Selah)

Notice how once David confessed his sin he felt forgiven and free. He was no longer bound by the sin. It does not matter what the sin was, the important thing is to acknowledge any transgression in order to receive a release from sin and receive forgiveness. Next, the Holy Spirit leads us to a place of cleansing and forgiveness in order to prepare us to draw closer to the Lord God. The Lord desires to show us His presence. Finally, through prayer, confession, and praise the Lord begins spiritually to bring us into His throne room. While meditating on the Lord, we started reflecting on H-is majestic wonder. He is truly awesome and glorious is His name. The Lord God is Holy, wonderful, magnificent, worthy, glorious, mighty, gracious, merciful, and from everlasting to everlasting.

As I think about the Holy Spirit the Lord impressed upon my heart, "Mighty Warrior." While praising Him with these words I cried with a heart of repentance. Repentance is choosing to turn away from sin and humbly turning to Jesus who is the author and finisher of our faith. Turning to Jesus is an act of surrender to follow Him. He tells us to fix our eyes on Him, who, for the joy set before Him endured the cross (Hebrew 12:1 -4). Surrendering ourselves to the Lord is a turning point for us as to whether we will submit to God or not (Our Daily Bread, 2007). It is the Holy Spirit who lives within us, who teaches

God In My Coffee

us how to turn from sin and reminds us to focus our thoughts on Him (Hebrew 3:1). He wants us to learn how not to look at our circumstances and be tempted to sin. Instead He wants us to turn to Him and let Him direct our path (Proverbs 3:5-6). Confessing our hurts, pains, and sin bring about another blessing; the Lord exchanges our sadness for His oil of gladness (Isaiah 61:3).

It is very hard to talk about how wonderful the Lord is without realizing how low we are as sinners. There is nothing we can bring or offer except a repentant heart because the Lord created everything. There is no room for self-righteousness. The Lord God is our righteousness and we are hid in Christ. The Lord uses our prayer time to cleanse our hearts and purge sin out. As we come He cleans us just as the Lord did with the prophet Isaiah. When Isaiah realized he had sinned he said, "Woe is me, I am a sinner" (Isaiah 6:5).

Cleansing comes from daily prayer, praise, confession, and repentance. As we open or surrender ourselves to Jesus daily He will show us little by little the things that we need to confess and repent. Whatever sin He brings to your mind, confess it and repent of it. Repentance means turning away from sin. The Lord God is faithful and just and He desires to restore fellowship with us on a daily basis. If we have sin it becomes difficult to have fellowship with the Lord because we will feel ashamed. But God is not a God of condemnation BUT an Eternal God of Love. He is Love and He comes to us in love. He loves us so much that through daily prayer He

God In My Coffee

draws us to Himself with a sweet peaceful love that goes beyond explanation. Believe me, this is how He works in my life and the way He will work in yours.

Every morning pray and praise Him, wait for Him to bring to your mind any sin (large or small) that may have committed (conscious or unconscious) and then bring it before Him. Then confess, repent, and pray for His forgiveness. He immediately forgives and remembers my sin no more, as far as the east is from the west (Psalm 103: 12).

One of the things I had been asking the Holy Spirit for was spiritual understanding about – forgiveness. He impressed on my heart a definition for forgiveness. It means releasing the debts or wrongs that you believe someone else may owe you. Whatever is troubling us, – GIVE IT to the Lord. The Lord God stands and waits FOR us to GIVE it to Him and He forgives us any debt or wrong and forgets it forever as far as the east is from the west. We all know the term but how do we apply this forgiveness to ourselves and others? We are to forgive, whatever debt, offense, wrong, or trespass that we or someone else may be holding onto – give it to the Lord God. As we go through this daily process of giving our debts and the debts of others to the Lord, the Holy Spirit removes it. This is His cleansing process. He is cleaning out our spiritual cup so that we may receive more of Him. Our job is to believe that the debt has been removed; we are now clean and are available to receive from Him.

As the Lord God prepares us for service to do His plan and purpose He has to clean and purify

God In My Coffee

our hearts. When He exposes the sin that so easily besets us or tempts us then He brings us to a place of repentance where we confess our sin and desire to turn away from it. The beauty of this process is, we can not turn from sin on our own. We need the Holy Spirit, the Lord of Host, the Mighty Warrior, to fight this battle for us. All we do is confess it, repent of it, and the Lord of Host fights the battle. This kind of sin is so deep to the point where we are not aware of what it is, yet we know when we feel the guilt, and shame of it. For example, in my life the sin that was impacting my life was fear – of man and trying to please man.

Each one of us has to repent and choose who we will follow and have a relationship with. In this situation we're not talking about salvation because you have already accepted Jesus as our Savior. What we're asking you—is whether Jesus is Lord of your Life. As Lord, are we willing to submit to His way, word, and life? Not only is Jesus our Savior He wants to be Lord of our lives and to have a relationship with us. This relationship comes as we finally make the "Jordan River" decision in our lives. David Wilkerson in His book "Hallowed Be They Name" (2004) talks about how once we cross the "Jordan" in our lives the Holy Spirit removes self-sufficiency and no longer do we have confidence in our flesh or ability. The Lord desires to show us a more excellent way.

Each one of us has a root sin that has become or can become a snare and hindrance to walking with Jesus. If we say we do not sin we lie. Many Christians

God In My Coffee

walk around feeling self-righteous and somewhat pious by observing and judging the sins of others. We must all stop, be quiet, and wait upon the Lord. As we wait and trust God He will gently and lovingly bring sin to the forefront. In order to go higher by faith in Christ we must acknowledge sin and have a repentant heart. Well, He showed me – FEAR.

If we don't think we have sinned then we won't believe we need to repent of anything. Each of us has a sin that distracts us from following Jesus. Sin can be very tricky. It creeps in before we know it, like the subtle little foxes or temptations in our lives. The first and most important step is to acknowledge sin in our lives. We all sin and if we are honest, God will dig deep into us to the root of the sin if we allow Him. He is able to deliver and heal us once and for all. Sometimes we have to unlearn some old behaviors that tempt us to sin again. I know this may be a difficult problem but it is much needed and we will feel better when sin is confronted and we are freed.

So go put your coffee pot on because we may need to sit a spell for this. This conversation is between you and God. If He wants you to go and talk with someone regarding fear, wait for Him to put the name of the person on your heart that you may need to talk with. For now, have a seat and get your coffee cup. God wants to pour himself into the coffee of your life this day and start the healing process to set you free from fear. The Lord God loves us so much He does not want us bound to old sinful ways. The Lord is just waiting for us to come and draw near to Him. He disciplines and sets free those who He loves

(Hebrew 12:9). When the Lord sets you free you are free indeed (John 8:36). It's time for freedom in your life.

Answer the following questions.
It between you and God

How much burden were we made for to carry?	Do you believe God can handle you burdens?
How often do you really give God your burdens?	When are the times you think God can't handle your burdens?

Well, here is a little of my testimony of how the Lord delivered me from the sin of fear. Don't forget, sometime deliverance is a process. Don't get frustrated, trust God and He will bring you all the way through. I know He will because He did that with me and He is no respecter of persons. I was on my way to work the day after Labor Day singing praise and worship songs in the car while driving through the heaviest part of my commute and there it was, spiritually right in front of me – fear. The prophetic word that came at church the day before was, to come out from under doubt and fear. While meditating on this word I asked the Lord to show me if this was true. In

God In My Coffee

God's grace and mercy He showed me that a spirit of fear had been present for many years. Matter of fact, when I accepted the Lord as my personal Lord and Savior in 1977, after reading a pamphlet, my best friend gave me a small Bible. The first scripture I looked up in the concordance section of that small Bible was about fear. It referred me to the Book of Psalms chapter 34. In this psalm King David talks about fear. In chapter 34:4 David writes, "I sought the Lord and he heard me and delivered me from ALL my fears." What I learned while reading about David was that he also had fears. If he did not he would not have talked about it. What I also realized was he kept moving forward trusting God even when the enemy was trying to use fear to spiritually attack him. The Book of Psalms is a great place to learn how to trust God and be delivered from fears, hurts, oppression, bondage, and sin in general.

David not only believed God as His deliverer, he also saw and focused on the goodness of God. In verse 7 it says the angel of the Lord encamps about them that fear the Lord and He delivers them. Fearing the Lord God is a reverent fear for the Almighty God, creator of heaven and earth. One thought that the Lord impressed upon my heart related to fear, our fears are usually related to losing something or someone; feeling threatened; or being rejected by someone who seems to be very important in your life. This type of fear means that we are too attached to a person or thing that has become very important to us – to the point that it is more important to us than God. As aforementioned, whatever becomes important to us we seek out and spend time doing things related to it. When we get too attached and overly protective or concerned about losing it, then fear creeps in and the object could become an idol to us. God desires that we seek Him and get attached to Him. He is a jealous God and He does not want us to put anything or anyone before Him. In Psalms 34:9 the Lord gives us the answer: fear the Lord, all believers, for there is no want for them that fear (reverence) Him. Fear God and not man or material things.

How wonderful it is to believe and acknowledge that the Lord God of Host delivers us from ALL of our fears. He sends His angels to camp around about us. I've read this many times, but this time I finally believed the Lord delivered me from the sin of fear that has, in the past, so easily entangled me. This time I believed and received freedom. To be honest, it's also comforting to know that the great King David also had fears and just like me he was delivered, as we can. David resolved the fear problem by saying, "Oh taste and see that the Lord is good. Blessed is the man that trusts in Him." Satan wants us to focus on our fears and doubts rather than on the goodness of God. It's amazing that dealing with fear and tasting God goodness are in the same chapter. It shows how big a problem fear is. God wants us to quickly give fear to him and He will restore and deliver us.

Usually fears are birthed during our early years in life. Fears keep us from moving forward and trusting God. Fear also tries to rob us from having the joy of the Lord. Therefore, deliverance from fear (for example in my life) takes place little by little

God In My Coffee

as I trust God. Each day we need to cast our cares and fears on the Lord and trust and thank God for being our deliverer. David, being a man after God's own heart, perceived God as mightier than his fear and trusted God continually to deliver him from his battles. King David viewed God as the great Lord God of Hosts who fights for us – because the Battle is the Lord's – not ours. Our job is simply to trust that God is in control. He is El Elyon, the Lord God, Creator of heaven and earth and El Shaddai, The Lord God All Sufficient, and He will do what He said He will do. He is the Lord God Almighty who we can truly depend on for deliverance. Even if all else fails – God Almighty can not. His promises are true. We just must believe He is who He said He is.

There were many other scriptures I held onto over the years related to being delivered from my fears: I Timothy Chapter 1 verse 7 is one I quoted for years – "God did not give us a spirit of fear; but of power, love and a sound mind." Now, I realize the Lord used these scriptures to sustain me until I was spiritually mature and ready for my deliverance.

I had been afraid of people even since childhood. As a child I pulled back from people. But God, in all of His grace and mercy and lovingkindness, took away my fear and restored my soul. The Lord God of Host is pulling down the walls of Jericho in my life. He showed me my fears and I immediately felt sadness and a heart of repentance. But, this was the day of my – healing, deliverance, and restoring of my soundness of mind. Only the power of His Spirit heals, mends, delivers, and restores our souls. I share

God In My Coffee

this because I know the truth set me free and hopefully will help you to cross over your Jordan and allow the Lord God to manifest His love for you in a new refreshing way to bring your wall down. Not only was the Lord bringing down a wall, He was also removing a mountain of fear in my life. I felt like the Lord was telling me – I'm turning up the heat in you life. The burner is up high because I am purging the old and making all things new.

Accepting God's love brings us to a place of security and safety. He helps us progress toward letting go and forgiving the offenses of others. Coming in contact with and sharing relationships with others– in marriage, at home, job, and even in the church, can be very challenging. In marriages husbands and wives can be easily offended because one or the other person did not do what their spouse expected. There are many times when I am reminded not to be offended. But offenses will come and if we react to them and get defensive or negative we block our own blessing. If not recognized – negativity can lead to anger, bitterness, unforgiveness and resentment. However, as we spend with the Lord, the Holy Spirit teaches us not to be offended. Jesus died on the cross for all negative offenses and evil feelings in the world. He already paid the price and forgave us – in advance – for all our sin. We have to accept His forgiveness, believe it, and forgive ourselves and others.

As we walk in love with the Holy Spirit we should put on mercy, loving kindness, and be tenderhearted with one another instead of being offended

(Colossians 3:12). Especially for the body of Christ, we should have patience and mercy with each other because God is working in all of our lives. It is the love of God that constrains us and God's love covers a multitude of sins (I Peter 4:8). The servants of the Lord must not argue but be able to teach and be patient with all men (2Timothy 2:24). Taking offense is emotionally expressing that we feel we have been wronged which means we think we have some form of righteousness. No, we have all fallen short. It's as if Jesus says, "Those who have not sinned cast the first stone". We all have sinned. The Holy Spirit teaches us not to sin. Every hour and minute of every day we choose how we will react and respond to situations. Situations will come. They come primarily to test and determine our mindset. Our job is to forgive and love the Lord God with all of our heart, soul, mind, and strength and to love one another. We also must learn to trust and believe that the Lord will do what He said He will do. Each one of us is made from dust and is very fragile. We have to be cautious of becoming offended because the next moment we may be offending someone else. Taking offense blocks our blessings because we can't hold a grudge and a blessing at the same time. There is not room for both. Offenses can also become a hindrance and a snare to what God is trying to work out for our good. The Lord says to be slow to anger and quick to listen. He desires to strengthen us in the inner man through the power and might of His Spirit. It is His strengthening that helps us to become less offended. Philippians chapter 1:6 says God is doing a good

God In My Coffee

work and will complete it. Trust that God is working it all out for good (Romans 8:28). In many cases He uses offenses as training opportunities to respond God's way instead of our old way so that His blessings can flow.

For years I had been a person who did not want to rock the boat. I would gingerly move about trying not to make any waves. Even though I had desires and aspirations of my own I would quietly work on my goals while trying not to offend and worry about what others would think of me, if I did not do what they wanted. It was as if I was living two lives. Being honest, I did not realize it but I was being double minded. I was more concerned about what people thought, and tried to please others and God at the same time. But the truth is that I was trying to please man more than God. Sometimes we need to be real in order to be finally free once and for all. Well, my two lives – physical and thought life – came to a head.

The Lord showed me how sometimes while praying on my knees I would jump up and get back in the bed if I thought someone was coming into the bedroom and I did not want them to feel uncomfortable. When the Lord showed me this, in a loving and forgiving way, it was as if He said to me, "Who are you going to please, man or me? Choose you this day who you will serve." The Lord says in Colossians Chapter 3:23, "Do it heartily unto the LORD and not unto men. Even though I had been delivered from fears in many areas of my life; this one last mountain had to be faced. When it got to the point where I jumped up from praying because someone was coming into the bedroom that was it: No more. It was time to stand up in the power of the Holy Spirit and first ask for repentance and second, speak up to the matter.

I had to confess my sin and confront the issue of what others might think. No more, that's it! I have decided to follow Jesus no matter what, no turning back and I must be obedient to what God has called me to do. Each person is responsible and accountable for their own actions. I choose to please God first. If man is also pleased – Praise God. The point is that my focus is on God and not man. God has delivered me from ALL my fears. The Lord replaced my fears with His love, power, and soundness of mind (I Timothy 1:7). That's something to shout about.

I would imagine that there are a lot of people reading this right now who want to come out of a fearful state of mind and replace it by receiving God's power, love and sound mind. Notice, the only thing that I had to do in order to come out of a "fear" frame of mind was to honestly repent and receive what God had for me. It's our choice. Fear and doubt can have such a strong hold on us that it is paralyzing. Well, it's our choice if we want to move from fear to love. Matter of fact, in I John, we are reminded that God's love casts out all fear. The Lord desires to free us from all our fears, concerns, and doubt. Jesus came to set the captives free. I only use myself as an example to reveal how you can be set free, just as I was.

As we face our walls or strongholds with a repentant heart, God intervenes. It is God's Spirit who tears down the walls in our lives. It is not we who

God In My Coffee

battle strongholds in our lives but the Holy Spirit. Our job is to pray, praise, and trust God, that He will do what He said he will do. Once we cross over our Jordan and the walls come down we walk in the new land with the Holy Spirit. We must walk with Him in order to be victorious in this new land of our heart. The Lord says:

Scripture Promise: Matthew 11: 28-30

Come unto me *ALL* you that labor and are heavy laden, and
I will give you rest; Take my yoke upon you and
LEARN OF ME For my yoke is easy and my burdens are light

Chapter Worksheet:

Look at the Spiritual Growth worksheet at the end of this chapter and use it to write down your personal notes. Write down how you feel right now and what you think the Lord is trying to show you. You may be going through difficulties or trials. Write that down. When you write it down, the mystery is taken out of the situation and the enemy can't hold these over your head anymore. When you confess thing that are in your heart and start praising God out loud it puts confusion in the enemy's camp. The enemy (Satan) He gets mad and flees because he can not stay around when God is being worshipped. Write down what you think the Lord has been trying to teach or show you while you have been reading this chapter. Then write down the suggestions He reveals that helps you to be triumphant from this time forward. One reminder the Lord gives me is: All fear is gone and the enemy is "under my feet."

Fill out the worksheet based on areas the Lord is working on in your life

TRIALS, TRAINING, AND TRIUMPH THROUGH TRUSTING GOD
TRIALS: 1.   2.   3.   4.
TRAINING AREAS: 1.   2.   3.   4.
TRIUMPHANT OPPORTUNITIES: 1.   2.   3.   4.

© 2008 Developed by Sherry B. Scott

CHAPTER FOUR:

GROWING IN GOD'S LOVE: ARE YOU A SEEKER?

Seek ye first the Kingdom of God and His righteousness

Matthew 6: 33

Meditating on the Word (Jesus) of God is like dwelling in *an ocean of God's living word.* The Lord gave me a picture of the Word of God – a vast ocean full of the living word. It was so large you could not see the end of it. Meditating on the word is like diving in daily, swimming and learning all about the Lord God through experiencing His word. Allow the Holy Spirit to take you places, spiritually, that He wants you to see and experience in the word. In this place you never grow tired and it is not a chore. The more you dive in the more you want to spend time there. Recently, I went snorkeling in the Pacific Ocean on Tortuga Island in Costa Rica, Central America. The ocean was so large yet when I was snorkeling the Lord was showing me the beauty of the clear blue ocean while I was looking under water. The more I relaxed and rested the more He showed me. While I was snorkeling I began worshipping the Lord in the beauty of His Holiness. Just like snorkeling the Lord desires to show us His vast beauty and reveals His promises as we dwell on the Word of God. It becomes the place where you dwell day and night – meditating on the Word of God. It's the place you want to be.

Scripture Promise: Psalm 1: 1-3

Blessed is the man that walks not in the counsel of the ungodly,
Not stand in the way of the sinners, not sit in the seat of the scornful.
But his delight is in the law of the Lord; and in His law does he meditate on it night and day.
And he shall be like of tree planted by the rivers of water that brings forth fruit in his seasons his leaf shall not wither, and whatsoever he does shall prosper

This sweet fellowship is the same original communion that Adam had with the Heavenly Father in the Garden of Eden. Adam and God communed

God In My Coffee

together daily in the cool of the day. Adam knew God. He recognized God's voice and spent time daily with him. The fellowship was broken when Adam and Eve were tempted by Satan, disobeyed God, and ate the forbidden fruit. Satan has been using the same strategy of doubt and temptation for thousands of years to keep us from praying and worshipping God. The enemy does not want us to read the word of God and know our real purpose in life – that of loving and worshipping the Heavenly Father who longs to draw us to Himself. Jesus was the only one who was able to break this curse that separated God and man. God used His only son Jesus to bring us back to Him. Jesus came to earth in the form of a man, suffered, was crucified, died, took the keys to death and Hell from Satan, rose again, and made a way for all mankind to be reunited with our Heavenly Father again.

As we spend more time with the Lord we begin desiring more and more time with Him. We realize that our heavenly Father is more real than our natural father. Matter of fact, we get to the point where we don't want to do anything to disappoint or disobey our Father because it would be displeasing. Obedience is no longer a chore but a willingness to submit to His way, truth and life.

I recently saw a John Bevere DVD about "Freedom from Sin" (2005). In one section of the DVD he referred to communing with our Heavenly Father through the Holy Spirit. John chapter fourteen says, "if you love me you will keep my commandments." This scripture means the more you fall in love with the Lord God and spend time with Him the more you want to obey His commands. Bevere explains this scripture no longer feels like a law or command but a relationship and desire to please God. We truly were His from the beginning before we were form in our mother's womb and before we were born. We are put on this earth "as a loan." The Holy Spirit guides us back to our first love, Jesus (Revelation 3:20). The Holy Spirit reunites us with our heavenly Father. Through the Holy Spirit we can commune and have fellowship with our Heavenly Father each day (*as Adam did in the beginning during the cool of the day*). The Lord God is our heavenly father but just like the earthly father in the prodigal son story, so our heavenly Father waits for us to return and come back to him (Luke 15: 11-32). He longs to fellowship and commune with us. We are the apple of His eye. He wants to talk with us and spend time with us. He truly will never leave nor forsake us. Wow, what a revelation.

The Lord promises through His word that if we return to Him, He will show us a love which we have never experienced before. The Lord will restore our souls and show us His path of righteousness. He will give us rest and make us lie down in green pastures. He says to come unto Him and He will give us rest for our souls (Matthew 11: 28 – 30). He will anoint our head with oil and our cup will overflow. The Lord constantly wants to fill our spiritual cups with more of Him. In the book of II Corinthians chapter four the Word says "for which cause we faint not: But though our outward man perish, yet the inward

God In My Coffee

man is renewed day by day" (II Corinthians 4: 16). Therefore we do not need to get frustrated, just *enjoy the journey*. This renewal process is ongoing: Purging out the old self and infilling us with the new spirit man – by the Holy Spirit. Those who believe in The Lord God through Jesus Christ our Savior, out of his or her spiritual heart (or belly) will now flow rivers of living water (which is His word). The Lord God will be an everlasting spring of life for our souls (John 7:38).

The Lord is a rewarder of those who diligently seek Him

Hebrews 11:6

Seeking God Through Prayer

One of the best ways to spend time and seek God is through prayer. Prayer is simply talking to God. We communicate with God by our **A.C.T.S.**: Adoration (praise and worship); Confession (of our sins); Thankfulness; and Supplications (expressing our needs and desires). Through prayer and meditation the Lord teaches me to be very sensitive to listening to the Holy Spirit's prompting to pray. When we pray, it must be in the name of Jesus Christ. It is through His shed blood, resurrection power, and authority that we even have a desire or unction to pray. On our own, we may not naturally seek the Lord. The Holy Spirit puts the desire or need to pray in our hearts. There is great power in prayer. Therefore, we should not

God In My Coffee

grow weary in praying. Prayer should be continuous, without doubting, and without vain repetition but by faith believing that God will answer in His time.

I was raised Catholic. I went to Catholic grade school and high school. My mother took us to church every week so praying was a common practice. I also observed my mother praying. While growing up I remember quietly watching my mother pray on her knees almost everyday. She never pushed her beliefs or mandated the family to get on their knees and pray. She just practiced what she thought was important. In the Catholic faith you learn several prayer by rote memory such as the Our Father, Hail Mary, and Apostles Creed. I had to memorize these prayers because it was my religion, but I did not have a relationship with the one to whom I was praying. I was praying out of requirement not out of love. I am realizing that religion is based on rules, laws and traditions and relationship is based on genuine love. Even though I was familiar with prayer I just did not understand the purpose of prayer. The Lord God wanted a relationship with me. I did not realize that prayer was really communicating with someone who you want to spend time with – God.

My mother was different from me, she understood and had a relationship with God. She knew how to pray and she spent time communicating with Jesus. My mother lived her entire life practicing the Catholic faith. She also was a born again Christian because she accepted Jesus as her personal Savior. Our religion does not make us a Christian. Only a relationship with our heavenly Father by accepting

God In My Coffee

Jesus Christ as our Lord and Savior allows us to be born again. Jesus paid the price and is the only way to eternal life with our heavenly Father. The wages of our sin is death, but the gift of God is eternal life in Jesus our Lord (Romans 6:23).

Over the years the Lord used my Catholic background and my mother's prayer habits to teach me that there is power in praying and seeking God. In 1978, I accepted Jesus as my personal Lord and Savior and the Holy Spirit moved into my heart. He taught me how to pray in the name of Jesus and how to talk to God on a more personal level. He reminds us through prayer to worship God, just because of who He is. In the late 70's my mother and I became involved in the Charismatic Movement. We both learned about the power of the Holy Spirit and being filled with the Spirit. The Holy Spirit encourages us to bring all of our hurts, concerns, and petitions to God. He also reminds us to have a heart of gratitude for all of the blessings that the Lord constantly bestows upon us.

The mere fact that you are breathing right now, probably had at least one meal, and have clothes on your back is enough reason to be thankful today. Prayer is very intimate and personal. As a mother of four children now I also kneel and pray daily because I want to spend time with my heavenly Father and know Him more each day.

Prayer is personal communication between you and God. He is always listening. He wants us to be honest because He knows everything that is happening and He knows our needs and desires. Many times He is just waiting for us to express them. Just because you may not have received an answer to prayer when you think you should have does not mean that God did not hear your prayer. Delays are not denial of our prayers. While we are waiting for answered prayers the Lord gives us hope.

Scripture Promise: Psalms 42:6

Why art thou cast down, O my soul?
And why art thou disquieted in me?
Hope thou in God for I shall yet praise Him
For the help of His countenance.

Hope is an act of faith, being sure that what you believe for shall come to pass, even though you do not see it yet (Hebrews 11:1). While you are waiting for God's promises to be manifested in your lives sometimes all you have is hope. Many men and women in the Bible had to wait for a long time for their promises. Jeremiah wrote: "Blessed is the man (or woman) who hopes (trusts) is in the Lord; whose confidence is in Him. He will be like a tree planted by the water." The Lord says that if we have no hope our hearts become sick; but a longing fulfilled is a tree of life (Proverbs 13:12). The Lord God gives us dreams and visions to keep us going while we are waiting and preparing for the future. This is when new and great opportunities are birthed. Sometimes, hoping and waiting signifies the end of one season and the beginning of something new.

Proverbs chapter 29:18 says, "where there is no vision, the people perish." Even the Lord God

God In My Coffee

is waiting and hoping that we will believe, accept, and follow Him so that He can bless us with more gifts and promises. The Lord God is our hope. In the Psalms He reminds us to put our hope in Him and He will bring it to pass in due season. Hope that is seen is not hope – but if we hope for that we have not seen; then do we with patience wait for it (Romans 8:25).

Scripture Promise: Romans 8:28

And we know that *ALL* things work together for good to them that love God, to them who are the called according to His purpose.

Over the years, I have learned that unanswered prayers does not mean failure but it usually means that God is still working things out for my good and in many cases He is teaching godly attributes and strengthening us. For example, while I wait, He renews our strength and teaches us how to trust Him.

Scripture Promise: Isaiah 40:30-31

The Lord is the everlasting God
The Creator of the ends of the earth
He will not grow tired or weary and
His understanding no man can fathom.
He gives strength to the weary and
Increases the power of the weak....

God In My Coffee

> But they that wait upon the Lord shall renew
> their strength
> They shall mount up with wings as eagles,
> They shall run and not grow weary. They
> shall walk and not faint.

Isaiah 40:31 has been my anchor verse for many years. Many times the Lord reveals Himself to me through songs and dreams. Several years ago the Lord gave me a dream that has sustained me while I have waited on Him. In this dream there was a mighty eagle with His wings spread flying from one mountain peak to another and I was tucked under His wings. As we were flying I felt very safe and peaceful. I could see the other mountain peak however I woke up before we got to the other side. Over the years I have remembered and thought about this dream. The Lord impressed on my heart that as I trust Him we go to the other side. Well, over twenty years later, the Lord again impressed on my heart that now we have reached the other mountain peak and now I am walking and following Him in the power of the Holy Spirit. Following Jesus through His Spirit is a life-long process. As we trust and wait on the Lord He reveals and gives us the desires of our heart.

Scripture Promise: Psalm 37: 3-4

> Trust in the Lord and do good
> Dwell in the land and enjoy safe pasture
> Delight yourself in the Lord and
> He will give you the desires of your heart.

God In My Coffee

Notice in this scripture that our part is to trust in the Lord and do good. Sometimes we want to skip over the verse that tells us what to do and then become inpatient when we don't think the Lord is giving us the desires of our heart. As we spend time praying and worshipping God we begin noticing that our delights and desires start matching up with His plan and desire for us.

I'll be honest and say I have been waiting for answers in certain areas of my life for years. But I also know that while I wait God gives me His love, peace, joy, presence, strength and comfort through His Spirit. I would not have it any other way because I would not be strengthened in the inner man with discipline and self control had He not taught me how to wait. However, while waiting, I am spending time and growing in the things of God by reading His word, meditating, and worshipping God through prayer.

Seeking God Through His Word

Another way we demonstrate our love for God is through seeking the Lord through His word. Those who love the Lord seek Him. And those who seek Him spiritually begin seeing God work in their lives. He truly is love, and the lover of our soul. If you believe He is the lover of your soul then you will seek Him. Matthew 6:33 describes how the Lord desires us to live. It says "seek first the Kingdom of God and His righteousness and all these other things shall be added." Notice what it does not say. It does not say seek after things because we just have to have them. In today's society there are so many technological breakthroughs such as small handheld communication devices, cellphones, laptops and of course the internet. We have so much available to us for instant gratification that we have forgotten how to earn or wait patiently for things.

The world is into quick microwaving, the Lord is into marinading. The enemy has tricked man into believing we just have to have this or that. Not only does the world mentality promote – get it now or if you're not happy with it – get rid of it, we have a tendency to put the cart before the horse, seeking the thing and not the Lord. This mentality is not just about things but also, sometimes, it's how we treat others in our marriages, job, and family. If we are not happy then get a divorce. People with a world mentality are not seeking God first because they don't believe what the word says or don't believe it applies to today.

Scripture Promise: Psalm 119: 103, 105

How sweet are thy Words unto my taste
Yea sweeter than honey to my mouth.
Thy Word is a lamp unto my feet and
A light unto my path

God knows what you need and want before you ask him. He knows the secret things in your heart. The Lord God is truly all sufficiency and all knowing (El Shaddai) such that He can give us all so much

God In My Coffee

more than our hearts can contain. Matter of fact, He says, "Call upon me and I will show you great and might things which you know not" (Jeremiah 33:3). He says "as you seek me you will find me when you search for me with all of your heart" (Jeremiah 29: 11 - 12).

Because God is love, He pursues us. But we have to believe He is truly there and truly cares for us. The Lord's love for us is so great that He will not force himself on us. He actually says simply "ask, seek, and knock." As we submit ourselves to him and draw near to Him He draws near to us. Knowing the Lord comes through reading God's word. As we read, God's Spirit teaches us how to follow Jesus' example and walk in love. In life we seek out those things we value and consider important. If it's valuable we spend time with it almost everyday. It could be enjoying music, reading a book, exercising, or looking up things on the internet. All of these things are good but the Lord desires that we put Him first and seek out His wonders, promises, fruits, and gifts. He actually says in Psalm Chapter 8, "taste and see that God is good."

What God offers daily is of supreme value. It's not a one time offer. We can have more and more every day, if we only believe and receive. When Moses turned towards the burning bush he was turning towards God, demonstrating a pursuit towards something greater than himself – The Great I AM THAT I AM. Moses turned with curiosity. The Lord still demonstrates His love towards each of us daily, we just need to notice with curiosity and turn toward

God In My Coffee

Him. When we do, that's the very moment we will taste and see that He is good.

Right now as you sip your coffee or tea He has put a curious thought in you heart. It's actually been there for a while but the distractions around us have been so loud that we didn't take the time to listen to His still small voice. However, God's love is so great and it is not too late to turn towards that curiosity nudging in your heart (spirit) right now. Matter of fact, put your cup down, stop reading and take a few quiet moments to listen to God right now. Ask God, "Lord have you been pursing me? Help me to listen right now." Then take time to learn of Him – dive into His word.

Seeking God Through Worship

Worship is displayed in many ways. The Lord desires to teach us how to worship Him in spirit and in truth through His Holy Spirit. The Holy Spirit will show us how to worship the Lord, our heavenly Father. Most people assume that worship is primarily through music. The words and motive of the song make it worship. This is not the only form of worship. In the Book of John Chapter 4 Jesus says in verse 23, "But the hour comes and is now, when the true worshippers shall worship the Father in spirit and in truth. The Father seeks those who worship Him. Since God is a Spirit and they that worship Him must worship Him in spirit and in truth." Jesus also said in John chapter 9 verse 31, "if any man be a worshipper of God, and does His will, He hears him."

This scripture reiterates that true worship is **doing** God's will. One way of learning and doing God's will is through reading and obeying His word. Obedience is a primary expression of worshipping the Lord. It is the natural outcome of spending time with the Lord God.

Scripture Promise: Psalm 138 1-3

I will praise thee with my whole heart;
Before the gods will I sing praise unto thee
    (O Lord)
I will worship towards thy holy temple, and
Praise thy name for thy lovingkindness and
    for thy truth;
For thou has magnified thy word above all
    thy name
In the day when I cried thou answer me and
Strengthened me with strength in my soul.

Daniel was a man committed to prayer and worship (Daniel Chapters 3). He sought the Lord daily – no matter what anyone else thought. His critics despised him for praying and worshipping. However, Daniel was more committed to the Lord God than to man, to the point that he was thrown into the fiery furnace. But God saved his life and his friends. The Lord sent the Son of God to be with them in the furnace. They were not harmed. Matter of fact, they did not smell like smoke, their clothes were not singed, and not a hair on their head was touched. They demonstrated a deep trust in God and worshipped Him. Their faith

God In My Coffee

was so strong that they believed God was mighty and able to deliver them. When they were delivered Daniel and his friends were promoted. They went through a firey furnace situation in their lives and received God's promotion and blessing.

We too are going through firey times. However, just like, Daniel, Joseph, Esther, Ruth, Job, and most of all Jesus, if we endure we will receive our promotion and blessing (Hebrews 12: 1-4). We must believe and remember that we don't go through difficult times alone. God is with us (Jehovah Shammah). He sent His Holy Spirit who lives within us, therefore Jehovah God is with us and He will comfort us with His rod and staff (Psalm 23:4).

It takes discipline and self-control to pray, read, and worship the Lord God. However, once you hear and see life from God's vantage point the other things of this world grow strangely dim. God's Spirit helps us to keep Him first and to put things into proper perspective so they don't become idols. Idols are anything that takes the place of God and become more valuable or important to you than Him. The enemy tries to reverse this and distract us with things that appear important but are only temporary and of very little value.

In 2006 I had the opportunity to travel to Sydney Australia to speak at an international health care conference. I have always wanted to visit this country. While there I had a strong desire to see the sunrise in the land down under. So one morning I got up at 4:00am, walked to the train terminal at 5:00am, took the train to the end of the line towards Bondi Beach,

God In My Coffee

proceeded to the bus terminal and took the bus to the end of its line to Bondi Beach, and asked the bus driver where to get off. The bus driver not only told me where to get off but he also told me where to stand to get the best camera shots of the sunrise. So I arrived at the location at 6:30am and waited.

Around 6:45am it started. The glory of God was revealed in the sunrise. I stood in awe of the Lord and thanked God for His sweet presence. After seeking Him out, He revealed the beauty of His holiness. I could see that He owns all things and creates all things. I experienced His presence, and paused to pray, praise, and worship the Lord. As aforementioned, we seek out those things or relationships that are important to us. Seeking Him in the sunrise was my desire. It was important to me to spend time learning about the wonder and majesty our God. Those who are diligently seeking the Lord God will be rewarded and are being set apart for His purpose.

CHAPTER FIVE:

SET APART FOR GOD'S PURPOSE

But know that the Lord has set apart him that is godly for Himself

Psalm 4:4

As we diligently seek our heavenly Father the Lord says "He has set apart those He calls His own." In Psalms Chapter 4, verses one to four, David describes how the Lord God sets apart those that are godly to Himself and He hears them when they call. If we commune with Him, he will hear us when we call. We stand in awe of Him and sin not. We commune with our own heart upon our beds and are silent.

Scripture Promise: Psalm 1-4

Oh you sons of men, how long will you turn
 my glory into shame?
How long will you love vanity and seek after
 false gods?
But know that the Lord has set apart him (her)
 that is godly for Himself:
The Lord will hear when I call unto Him.
Stand in awe, and sin not:
commune with your own heart upon your bed
 and be still

These verses offer a strategy of how we are to deal with difficult seasons of life. It's interesting how King David talks of God having set apart those who are godly unto Himself right in the middle of two verses that talk about adversities and the enemy trying to destroy us. Since David had spent quality time with God on a daily basis, he was prepared for difficult times. King David shares with us how it's in the quiet times with God that we learn to use strategies for when adversity comes. That why he could say in verse 2 directly to the enemy's face, "God sets apart those that are godly to Himself and hears them when they call." Then He says "Stand in Awe" of the Lord even though we may want to get angry and lash out towards the enemy. The Lord God instructs us in these times while we lay on our beds to "Be Still". Psalms 46:10 reads "Be Still and Know that I am God. I will be exalted among the nations and in the earth." In today's language it is as though the Lord is trying to say, "trust me, I am working *all* things out for *your* good and I will be exalted above the earth. I the Lord God Almighty am with you." The Lord tells us in His word to Trust Him. But do we trust Him to handle our circumstances?

> **Do we really trust that God can....?**
>
> **When are the times that you don't trust God?**

Once we realize that we can trust the Lord then He starts the healing and mending process through His flow of love and living water in our hearts. This process takes place when we come unto Him. He is waiting for us to tell Him all about how we feel. Only the Lord Jesus can mend and give us rest. He takes away the pain and hurt. Matter of fact, Jesus sent His Spirit to comfort and heal us. Remember, we have already accepted Jesus as our personal Lord and Savior and now the Holy Spirit lives within us. The Holy Spirit is waiting to hear your every cry, burden and pain. He wants us to lay it down at His feet by faith. Believe that He hears you. He gives His perfect peace and replaces your pain with His peace. He gives His perfect peace to those that keep their mind (spiritually) on Him (Isaiah 26:3). His peace surpasses anything you have ever experienced. Peace is the absence of fear. Rest is also found in His perfect

God In My Coffee

peace. As we trust and give our cares to the Lord He promises to give us His rest (Matt 11:28 – 30).

Communing with Jesus comes through yielding ourselves totally, submitted and surrendered. Surrendering is a daily process. As we let go of our self will and our way of doing things, and begin yielding to God's will, we begin dying to self daily, and start listening to the Holy Spirit's leading and guiding. As we draw near to Him, he draws near to us. We draw near by prayer, worship, and reading the word. The Lord desires that we dwell and abide with Him forever in the secret place of the Most High (Psalm 91:1). Another word for communing is dwelling.

Dwelling on the Lord is a secret place where the Lord strengthens, protects, shelters, and teaches. The Holy Spirit speaks to us there. He leads and guides us all truth, because He shall not speak of himself but whatsoever He hears (from the Heavenly Father), that is what He speaks and He will show you things to come (John 16:13). In addition each day the Lord renews our mind and cleanses us from all unrighteousness. Since the Holy Spirit resides in our hearts, He begins to clean and purify us. He gently convicts us of sin in our lives. Because God's great love is so gentle and kind He purifies those who belong to Him in order to draw us closer to Him. We don't have to be afraid as we come before Him daily. The Lord God is good and His mercy endures forever.

Refilling our spiritual cup

Knowing that I am forgiven, I continue seeking and communing with Him each day and wait for His Spirit to lead and guide me. As I read the word of God the Holy Spirit fills my cup with His love. Being set apart means we have liberty in Christ to receive our refilling each day of God living waters. One beautiful thought the Holy Spirit put in my spirit today is: It's time to walk with Him daily, to walk with the Lord God in the power of the Holy Spirit.

Scripture Promise: 2 Chronicles 16:9

For the eyes of the Lord run to and fro throughout the whole earth, strengthen those whose hearts are fully committed to Him.

The Holy Spirit is looking and waiting for us to acknowledge Him so that He can teach and lead us in the path of life. It's time to receive and commune with Him daily by listening to Him, waiting upon Him, trusting Him, loving Him, obeying Him, resting and waiting patiently for Him, and most of all dwelling with Him in the secret place of the Most High in order to delight ourselves in Him.

Spending time with the Lord brings us into His presence and in His presence is fullness of joy (Psalm 16: 9). His presence is His Holy Spirit that already lives within us and desires to manifest Himself in us if we let him. David Wilkerson in his book "Hallowed Be Thy Name" refers to the pres-

God In My Coffee

ence of God as His Shekinah glory (glorious light). Wilkerson wrote, "The Lord God, our Shepherd, is compelling us to follow Him into His rest, so that He might "shekinah" in our midst. As we dwell with the Lord God in the secret place of the Most High, we rest with Him.

As in the Old Testament when God's glory came down and rested in the Holy Temple made by man, now the Spirit of God resides in us and our bodies are the temple of the Holy Spirit. His shekinah glory and presence shines through us. Therefore we must not defile the temple of God for the temple is Holy. Holy means, "set apart" for the Lord's purpose. If you are a believer you belong to Him then God desires to set you apart for His glory. So let Him shine and work His will and purpose in you for His glory. God's presence and glory is manifested in us individually as we hear His voice in the cool of each day.

Meditate on the Word of God

As I meditate on the word of God, His Holy Spirit teaches me how to listen to the Lord. The Lord desires that we walk in His way. The only way to experience Him is to listen and seek Him. The Book of Deuteronomy teaches us how to walk in His way. Chapter 30 reminds us, through the children of Israel who are about to enter into the promise land, to choose life. This choice make us more sensitive to the Lord's ways and therefore we love God more and want to listen to His voice and hold fast to Him. In Isaiah 51:1 it is written; "Listen unto me you who

God In My Coffee

pursue righteousness and who seek the Lord. Listen to me O Jacob, Israel, whom I have called. I AM HE. I AM the First and the Last (Isaiah 48: 12). Listen unto me....Give ear and come to me, hear me that your soul may live. I will make an everlasting covenant with you (Isaiah 55: 2 – 3)."

David loved the Lord God with all of his heart, mind and might. Matter of fact, David is referred to as a "man after God's own heart." David wrote the Psalms. Reading this makes me realize how loving and meditating on the Lord increased David's desire to hear the Lord more. As our commitment and discipline grows towards seeking the Lord then we develop a sensitive heart and become more open to hearing the Lord's voice in our heart (Psalm 40:6 and John 10:27). In Deuteronomy 6: 1 – 4 the Lord also reminds us to tell our children about Jesus and the word of God.

Psalm 34:11 says– Listen to me little children; I will teach you the fear of the lord. Ultimately, we desire to do the Lord's will, His way. Revelation Chapter 3 reminds us "Let him that has ear to hear, let him hear." In Matthew Chapter 11:28 – 30 Jesus not only wants us to come unto Him but as we trust Him more and more He also wants us to learn of Him through the Holy Spirit. In order to break from old habits of the past, we have to unlearn old ways and learn of His new ways. I love the scripture that says "old things have past away, behold all things are new" (I Corinthians 5:17). Growing in God's love is realizing that we now have newness of life.

Newness of life comes from learning of Him (Romans 6:4). Newness comes from drawing near the Lord as He draws near to us (James 4:8). The Lord wants us to get to know Him through reading and meditating on His word. There is power in the word however, if you don't read the word you won't realize the there are many facets to the name of God. Each facet is truly a diamond of radiant light that enlightens our understanding of Him. The Holy Spirit freely gives wisdom and understanding of God character as we seek the Lord. The Holy Spirit also empowers us and manifest Himself through us to do God's will. If you don't know The Lord God by His character and the facets of His name then you miss out on the awesome power that He desires to reveal to us and demonstrate through us. As Jesus said to the disciples, "greater works then these will you do" (John 14:12). The Holy Spirit's enlightenment and empowerment reveals who God is through His multifaceted names and character.

At times, I read other versions of the Bible and Bible commentary books to help me understand the word of God. One book that talks about the names and character of God is Dave Wilkerson's "Hallowed Be Thy Name". Dave (2001) wrote the book to help believers gain a heart of knowledge about God's names. God revealed His names all throughout the Bible to meet people where they were, in times of crisis, and to move them to a higher level through receiving, believing, and trusting that God will do what he promised in His word. The following names describe God's nature: El Elyon "God Most High,

Creator and Possessor of Heaven and Earth, and He is still not creating in us everyday"; El Shaddai "God All – Powerful and All – Sufficient"; Jehovah Jireh "The Lord Who Sees and Who Provides"; Jehovah Rophi "the Lord Who Heals *and mends* You"; Jehovah Makkeh "The Lord Who Smites"; Jehovah Nissi "The Lord our Banner" – who is Jesus; Jehovah Tsebaioth "The *Mighty* Lord of Hosts" – (Mighty Warrior); Jehovah Shalom "The Lord Our Peace – *in times of crisis*; Jehovah Tsidkenu "The Lord Our Righteousness" – *there is nothing we bring but a repentant heart*; Jehovah Shammah "the Lord is There – *God's Shekinah Glory*; Jehovah Rohi "The Lord My Shepherd" – The Lord is my Shepherd I shall not want; Immanuel "God with Us"; His Name is Forgiveness "the God who Pardons"; and "Christ Our Intercessor". Each name reveals a facet of God character to His people by actually doing for us what he proclaims of himself to be, in our time of need – we all need Him daily.

Growing in Christ is a wonderful lifelong journey. It's wonderful because you begin realizing that you will never be alone again. God is with you as you go through life. One revelation that the Lord put on my heart recently was: As we go through life, with Christ, we will be tested first and then promoted. This analogy makes sense to me because as an associate professor a large university and right now the students are preparing for their final exams. Students realize that first they learn new material, then study in order to apply this new information. Well, the Lord does the same thing with His children (us). As we spend time reading His word we begin learning new knowledge about the Lord God. The Holy Spirit gives us wisdom and understanding when we ask for help in order to move the new information from head knowledge to heart understanding (James 1:5). Once we have it in our hearts then Lord will lovingly test us. When we are tested it does not always mean we have done something wrong.

In many cases, the Lord is strengthening us through the test so that we can grow more. Then He can promote us in areas where He desires to use us. We become ripe fruit ready for His service. Ultimately, He uses us to share with others about the gospel of Jesus Christ and how the Lord has touched our life. The Lord knows when we are ready to be promoted. We don't have to rush things. However, when the tests of life come, let's remember who God is and how He has touched our life and then through the power of the Holy Spirit let's pass the tests with flying colors. Many people in the Bible were promoted after their faith was tested and they went through trials, for example: Moses, Job, Joseph, David, Daniel, Esther, Ruth, and most of all: Jesus. Each persons' faith is tested. In the academic world students are tested in areas such as Math, English, languages, and psychology but God, lovingly tests our faith.

God In My Coffee

> **The Question:**
> The Lord gave me a question and strategy that I would like to share with you. Here is a question each of us has to answer one-on-one basis:
>
> **Is Jesus the Lord of your Life?**

L. O. R. D.

L = Listen: In order to follow the leading and guiding of the Holy Spirit we need to listen and hear the Lord spiritually. Jesus said "My sheep hear my voice, and I know them, and they follow me" (John 10:27) also; "whoever listens to me shall dwell in safely and shall be quiet from fear of evil" (Proverbs 1:33). Psalm 27:7 talks about David who cried out and asked the Lord to hear his cry and answer him. We need to know and seek the Lord in order to hear Him answer our cry.

O = Obey "If you love me you will keep (obey) my commandments" (John 14:13). It's not about us. "Not my will but thy will be done on earth as it is in Heaven."
John 15:9 "If you obey my commands. If you keep my commandments you shall abide in my love; even as I have kept my father's commandments and abide in His Love. These things I have spoken unto you so that **MY** joy might remain in you and your joy might be full."

God In My Coffee

Joshua 24:24 – "The Lord our God we will serve; and His voice will we obey." (Joshua was a man who had Jehovah God as the Lord of his Life).

R = Relationship (Rest and Wait on the Lord and Rejoice)

Isaiah 26:3 says "I will keep you in perfect peace if you only keep you eyes straight on me (the Lord)."
Isaiah 40:31 "They that wait upon the Lord shall renew their strength they shall mount up on wings as eagles they shall run and not grow weary walk and not faint." Being a follower of Christ requires willing submission to the Lord. Submitting your ways and thoughts help us line up with his ways.
James 4:7. "Draw near to him and you will draw near to us. At times He wants us to Wait in Silence" Psalm 46:10.
Psalm 27:14 – "Wait on the Lord, be of good courage, and He shall *strengthen your heart*, Wait I say on the Lord."

The Lord wants to have a **relationship** with us. This is a close and intimate relationship with Him. In the relationship he wants us to **TRUST, REST, AND WAIT ON HIM.** While we are resting and waiting on the Lord (whether you are in a spiritual, physical, or emotional prison) **Rejoice in the Lord.** This is what Paul did (Phil. 4:4). Paul was actually in prison while he rejoiced in the Lord. While you are waiting for the breakthrough in your situation **rejoice in the Lord** because the devil is a defeated foe.

D = Do God's will and Delight in Him. As we delight ourselves in the Lord and do His will He gives us the desires of our heart. Since we are delighting in Him our desires emerge into wanting to please Him.

God In My Coffee

Our Wonderful Lord

The Lord God desires that we get to know Him. A few scriptures for us to read and meditate on in the Word of God that describe how wonderful the Lord are:

- John 15:7 Jesus said 'if you abide in me and my word abide in you, then you ask what you want and it shall be given to you."
    - o Joshua abided in the Lord God. We to need to spend time with the Lord – because to love Him is to know Him.

- Psalm 1; Psalm 119; Proverb 3: 5 & 6, remind us how the Lord direct your path. If we know His word we will recognize His voice.- Spirit of Truth - the Holy Spirit: He only speaks what he hears His Father and Jesus say. Jesus is the Word therefore The Spirit speaks the words which are truth (John 14, Matthew 10:20, 27).
- Deuteronomy 6: 1-11: Tell your children and your children's children about the word of God

King David wrote in the Psalms, seek the Lord early. David sought the Lord God early in the morning. Jesus sought the Lord early, He would get away alone to the mountains to spend time with God. A few beautiful scriptures meditate on are:

God In My Coffee

- Psalm 146:7- Great is our Lord and of great power; His understanding is infinite
- Isaiah 55:8- For His thoughts are higher than our thoughts and His ways are Higher than our ways.
- Psalm 73:26- My flesh and my heart faileth but God is the strength of my heart and My portion forever.
- Verse 28- It is good for me to draw near to God. I have put my trust in the Lord God that I may declare His works.
- Isaiah 55:6- Seek ye the Lord while He may be found, call ye upon him while He is near.
- Joshua 1:5 As I was with Moses, so I will be with thee
- James 3:7- Submit yourself therefore to God, resist the devil, and he will flee from you. But, draw near to God and He will draw near to you (purify your heart)
- Psalm 77:13- So Great of a God is Our God. Thou art the God that does wonders. Thou has declared thy strength among the peoples.
- Psalm 139-14- I praise thee Lord because I am fearfully and wonderfully made, Marvelous are thy works; and that my soul knows right well.
- How precious also are thy thoughts unto me. O God how great is the sum of them.
- Verse 6- Such knowledge is too wonderful for me. It is too high. I cannot Attain unto it. I do not exercise myself in great matters, or in things too high For me.

- Deut. 29:29- The secret things belong unto the Lord our God. But those things which are revealed belong unto us and our children.
- Heb. 10:38- but my righteous ones will live by faith and when I shrink back God is not pleased. (Don't turn back because if you do you bring the past into the present and take away from your future blessings).
- Psalm 104:24- O Lord- how manifold are thy works; in wisdom has thou made them All the earth is full of thy riches.
- Psalm 119: 105- Thy word is the lamp unto my feet and the light unto my path.
- Psalm 121- I will lift up my eyes unto the hills from whence come my help. My help comes from the Lord who made heaven and earth. The Lord is my keeper. The Lord is thy shade upon the right hand. The Lord shall preserve thy going out and coming in from this time forth and even forever more.
- Psalm 91: 1-5- He that dwelleth in the secret place of the most High shall abide under the shadow of the Almighty...In Him will I trust…. He shall cover me with His feathers under His wings shall I trust; He is my shield and buckler…
- I Peter 5:7- The Lord loves us so much that He says: Cast *ALL* your cares on Him Because He cares for you

Take a few minutes to share your cares with the Lord.

Do you believe that God really cares about you? (Be honest)	Do you believe that he sent the His Holy Spirit to comfort, love, and guide you?
Do you believe that God is Real Love?	Do you believe that the Holy Spirit can really help you? Do you want help?

Oh Taste and See that God is good and His Mercy (Love) Endures Forever (Psalm 34:8)

CHAPTER SIX:

IT'S TIME TO WORSHIP GOD

Oh Worship the Lord in the Beauty of His Holiness

Psalm 96:9

Come, now is the time to worship. Take some time right now and remember how much God loves and desires to overflow you with His goodness and benefits. Psalm 103: 1-5 demonstrates how to think about the tender mercies and lovingkindness.

Scripture Promise: Psalm 103: 1 – 5

> Bless the Lord, O my soul and all that is within me bless His Holy Name. Bless the Lord, O my soul and forget not all His benefits.

God In My Coffee

> Who Forgives all (our) iniquities and heals all of our diseases
> Who redeems my life from destruction;
> Who crowns me with lovingkindness and tender mercies.
> Who satisfies my mouth with good things,
> so that my youth is renewed like the eagle

Ask the Lord to reveal one aspect of Himself to your heart. Put the coffee mug down for just a minute, close your eyes and Let Him whisper His word in your ear. This is between you and the Lord. No one knows. No one else can hear. If you ask and believe right now, He will manifest a characteristic of who He is. Listen, believe, and receive what He has for you right now. Amen.

Worship Promise Scripture: Psalm 96: 9

> Oh Worship the Lord in the Beauty of His Holiness

Worship is expressed throughout our daily lives – at work; at home; in our community and fellowship settings. The Holy Spirit teaches and guide us how to worship and do things God's way in good times and difficult times. When God is glorified people are drawn closer to Him and want to know more about Him. The more we believe that God is in control of our situations the more we obey what God calls us to do by faith. In Hebrews, the writer shares how the Israelites wandered in the desert for forty years and did not enter into God's rest because of their unbelief. Many of us wander and do not experience God's rest because we are trying to figure things out on our own or because of unbelief, doubt, and lack of trust we do not believe that God is able to handle things in our lives.

How we treat others demonstrates an attitude of Christ love. For example, when we encounter difficult situations we may choose to either demonstrate anger, bitterness, a sharp tongue, ungodly attitude or, we may rise above reacting in the circumstance and demonstrate the fruits of the Spirit. We may display love, patience, kindness, meekness, self control, longsuffering, love, faith, and peace (which are the fruits of the Spirit). It is not in our own strength that we do this. As we spend time with the Lord, the Holy Spirit teaches and empowers us to manifest these fruits of the Spirit. The Holy Spirit reminds us that His grace is sufficient for us. His strength is made perfect in our weakness (I Corinthians 12: 9 – 10). In my own strength I might find myself either pulling back or holding in anger. However, the Holy Spirit strengthens and asks us to give Him that anger and He will replace it with His love, peace, joy, meekness, and self control. Matter of fact, as we let go of trying to do it on our own the Holy Spirit begins to manifest what He can do in the situation.

When Moses hit the rock for water instead to speaking to the rock (which the Lord told him to do), he demonstrated his own strength and God was dishonored and not glorified and for this reason Moses could not enter into the promise land (Numbers 20:

6 – 12). We live to worship God. He absolutely will not share His glory with any man or woman. He will manifest His (Shekinah) glory in us through His Holy Spirit not our glory but His. Everything we say, do, and think should glorify Jehovah God and direct others to Him.

Worship is also a form of spiritual warfare. Psalm 149 talks about the high praises of God that binds the enemies' fetters. Worship puts confusion in the enemies' camp. Worship goes beyond us and is not concerned about what others think. Our Heavenly Father is seeking worshippers, those who will worship before the breakthrough or manifestation comes. We are to worship with a pure motive, not to gain something but because of *Who* God is. That's why many times you'll hear someone say to pray and worship in your quiet place because it's not about your getting attention but about worshipping in spirit and in truth with sincerity and dedication in our heart. Then you must believe He receives your praise. I Corinthians 10:31 says to do all to the glory of God.

People are going to worship something: themselves, other gods, or the Lord God Almighty. If we have no worship we have a dark mind. You'll know if you are living in sin and darkness when you can not worship God. Adam and Eve were aware of God's presence and spent time with God in the cool of the day. An example of a great time to meet with God is sundown or early mornings. God will not share His glory with any man. Herbert (2007) discusses that there were three things in the world before the fall of mankind: revelation (hearing God like Adam did in the Garden of Eden); marriage; and work.

These are the three forms of worship and where we are to give God the glory. Worship is intimate between you and the Father. It's falling in love with Jesus more and more while we're putting God first. Worship is a way of life. It is what we do, not who we are. As we learn to worship, even when things don't seem to be going well in our lives, the Lord God interjects a new song in our spirit to remind us He is still there (Jehovah Shammah) and that He loves us very much. Repentance and worship are the quickest way to God. In these last days the spiritual atmosphere has changed. We must redeem the times through prayer, praise, worship, reading and meditation on the word of God because the days are evil (Ephesians 5:17).

As we yearn for God's presence we desire to worship Him more and more. Worshippers receive revelation (spiritual understanding of God's word) because they have an open heart to hearing God through His Spirit. Worshipping is the key to growing and being strengthened in Christ. Paul and Silas worshipped in the midst of trials and testing and they saw miracles. After they were thrown into prison they praised and worshipped through song and God delivered them out of prison. When we are going through difficult times we should follow their example and pray, praise, and worship God. The Lord reminds us that it is His Spirit who brings us through trying times in our lives.

The writer of Hebrews describes a sacrifice of praise (Hebrews 13:14). In the verses the disciples were going through difficult times and feeling pressed. Take for example Paul. He spent a lot of time in prison, but that's where he wrote letters to the various churches. He wrote to the Philippians, and told them to rejoice always and again rejoice, even though he was in prison at the time. When I think about it, this is amazing. Think about what we do when we are hard pressed and stressed – whether at work or home. It's easy to worship on Sunday morning when everyone is singing great praise and worship songs. However, during the week when things get challenging we might get into a critical spirit and even blame others for the problems in our lives. This should not be. Truthfully speaking it's easier to gripe or complain about our situations. As children and disciples of Christ it's time to check these behaviors. Trials will definitely come – don't be surprised. Be ready for the trials. Trials are meant to question and strengthen us. If we can learn to obey God and worship Him during our trials then we can learn to trust God to sustain us and bring us through.

A wonderful friend, who recently passed away lived and demonstrated a beautiful example of worship with "simply joy." She displayed an inner joy with everyone she met and in everything she did, whether in good or bad times. She gave joy to others that was not based on feelings but came from the Holy Spirit. This joy is a manifestation of one of the fruits of the Spirit. One of her favorite scriptures was Psalm twenty-seven. The psalm begins

God In My Coffee

with describing the Lord God as our light, salvation and the strength of our life. In verse six, King David writes about offering a sacrifice of joy: "I will sing, yes, I will sing praises to the Lord." A sacrifice of joy is given because the psalmist trusts that God will bring him through. She exemplified the same joy. She trusted God to be her sustainer and be her joy. The psalm ends with a powerful verse of strength: "wait on the Lord, be of good courage, and He shall strengthen thy heart, wait, I say on the Lord." Simply joy was her motto and she spread it everywhere she went – like rose petals. It was not until her funeral that I realized that she left a rich legacy and blessing.

Scripture Promise: Psalm 27: 1, 6

The Lord is my light and my salvation whom shall I fear?
The Lord is the strength of my life; of whom shall I be afraid?
And now shall mine head be lifted up above my enemies round about me; therefore will I offer in His tabernacle sacrifices of joy; I will sing yes, I will sing praises to the Lord.

During difficult times one of the things the Lord is trying to teach us is who we are in Christ. We are children of the Lord Most High God. Because Jesus died on the cross for our sins and paid the price with His blood we can be adopted sons and daughters and joint heirs with Christ. The book of Ephesians does a wonderful job of reminding us who we are in Christ. In Chapter two Paul reminds us that we are saved by grace as we accept Christ as our personal Lord and Savior. We immediately become adopted and are members of the body of Christ. That's a little about who we are. If you read down just a little further in Ephesians Chapter two, verse eight, it tells you where we are. Spiritually, as children of God, we are seated with Jesus in heavenly places and we have all spiritual blessings available to us. It's up to us to believe and act on this. That means that while we are going through trials and tribulations we can choose to be of good cheer and worship the Lord because we are spiritually in heavenly places with Christ and above the circumstances in our lives.

Scriptural Promise: John 16: 33; Psalm 27:14

These things I have spoken unto you that in me you might have peace. In the world you shall have tribulation but be of good cheer; I have overcome the world.

Wait on the Lord, be of good courage, and He shall strengthen your heart; wait I say on the Lord.

I have been growing in Christ, learning to trust Him more and more in difficult times. Now, during each trial I actually choose in what way I will respond. I may quietly pray under my breath and ask the Holy Spirit for guidance. I turn my eyes towards Jesus when these situations occur and pray or talk

God In My Coffee

with him through the Holy Spirit and ask for guidance and counsel to get me through. I then wait for a couple seconds to hear God's response. I usually experience a peaceful, quiet reminder to be still and know that God is truly God and He is able. In First Peter Chapter 4 verse 12, Peter says, "don't think it strange concerning the fiery trial which is to try you, as though some strange thing happened to you. If you are insulted because of the name of Christ, you are blessed, for the Spirit of glory and of God rest on you." We don't respond in the world's ways. We do it God's way, choosing to realize that we can trust God to handle our circumstances. Our job is to trust, obey, and worship God during good or difficult times.

There are also many occasions during difficult times when I have to spiritually stand and be strong in the Lord and the power of His might (Ephesians 6:10 – 12). God's job is to handle the situation while my job is to trust Him. He is very capable and knows exactly what we are going through. Charles Stanley wrote; "God assumes full responsibility for enabling us to carry out the work He assigns." Engaging in work for the Lord includes trials. God will never leave us to accomplish any task on our own. Matter of fact, God actually said, "I will never leave you or forsake you" (Hebrews 13:5). God knows the beginning from the end. He promises that He will never put us in any situation without providing us an escape.

Scripture Promise: I Corinthians 10:13

There has no temptation taken you but such as is common to man; but God is faithful, who *will* not suffer you to be tempted above that you are able; but with the temptation also will make a away of escape; that you may be able to bear it.

One of our best examples of a person who worshipped God during trials and adversity is King David. David was living in caves to avoid the wrath of King Saul. But during the toughest times David wrote the Psalms. These Psalms are songs of worship. In Psalm 33 and 34 David starts each Psalm by singing praises to the Lord God. However in Psalm 34 David was fleeing from King Saul and he went to Gath. Afterward David realized that the people of Gath wanted to kill him so he acted insane in front of the king, so that the king would not think he was a threat and kill him (I Samuel 21: 10 – 15). It is intriguing to me how King David went through so many years of difficulty, but in those years he wrote the Psalms.

David was very afraid yet he praised and worshipped in the most unlikely times. His life was threatened for several years. However, during times of fear and threats on his life, he wrote psalms and worshipped God. In Psalm 34, David starts out by saying, "I will bless the Lord at all times: His praise shall continually be in my mouth. My soul shall make her boast in the Lord: the humble shall hear

God In My Coffee

and be glad. O magnify the Lord with me, and let us exalt His name together. I sought the Lord, and He heard me and DELIVERED ME FROM ALL OF MY FEARS... The Lord heard me and saved me out of ALL my troubles." The troubles David had were very severe, even life threatening. But he magnified, glorified, praised, sang, and worshipped God anyway and God delivered Him from all His fears.

Ultimately, David believed that God was able to rescue and deliver him. Let's be honest, we may not be at this level of walking and trusting God, but God is merciful. He desires that we all come to the place or time in our lives where little by little and day by day we trust God more and grow in faith believing that God is able to bring us to the intimate place of healing, renewal, and restoration.

Another example of this kind of faith is Paul and Silas when they were thrown into prison – yet at around midnight they began worshipping and praising Him (Acts 16:25). They believed God so much that they were able to praise and worship Him. The Lord delivered Paul and Silas out of prison through an earthquake. The guard thought the men had escaped and he was going to kill himself. But Paul and Silas were still there and used that opportunity to pray and lead the guard to accepting Jesus Christ as his Lord and Savior. Paul and Silas were freed and used this opportunity to minister to another person. It is very interesting to note that the more men and women in the bible believed (trusted) and obeyed God the more they worshipped God and ministered to others at what might seem the oddest times.

King David was known in the bible for being a man after God's own heart and interestingly enough King David wrote the most in the bible about praise and worship. He set the example of "how to" praise and worship God even through difficult circumstances. An example of one of the most beautiful Psalms is Psalm 96. Meditate on these words of how David worships the Lord God in the Beauty of His Holiness. These Psalms strengthen and renew us. They also remind us of the promises of God.

PSALM 96

O sing unto the Lord a new song:
sing unto the Lord all the earth
Sing unto the Lord, bless His name;
Show forth His salvation from day to day
Declare His glory among the heathen,
His wonders among all people
For the Lord is great, and greatly to be praised;
He is to be feared above all gods.
For all the gods of the nations are idols: but the
Lord made the heavens.
Honor and majesty are before Him:
Strength and beauty are in His Sanctuary.
Give unto the Lord, O you kindred of the people,
Give unto the Lord glory and strength
Give unto the Lord the glory due His name
Bring an offering, and come into His courts
OH WORSHIP THE LORD IN THE BEAUTY OF HIS HOLINESS
Fear before Him, all the earth
Say among the heathen that the Lord reigns:

> The world also shall be established
> that it shall not be moved:
> He shall judge the people righteously
> Let the heaven rejoice, and let the earth be glad;
> Let the sea roar, and the fullness thereof.
> Let the field be joyful, and all that is therein:
> Then shall all the trees of the wood rejoice
> Before the Lord for He cometh,
> for He cometh to judge the earth:
> He shall judge the world with righteousness,
> and The people with His truth.

As we worship the Lord God He gives us His presence which is fullness of joy (Psalm 16:11). Through worship He desires to show us the path of life; in thy presence is fullness of Joy. God also desires that we have His Presence, His Peace (Jesus is our Prince of Peace), and His Power (through the Holy Spirit). One way I worship the Lord daily in addition to prayer and reading the word – is through song. I enjoy singing and throughout most of the day I find myself meditating on a spiritual song. Ephesians Chapter five teaches us how the Lord desires that we sing songs, hymns, and spiritual songs in our hearts. These songs are given to us to strengthen us daily in our heart. They encourage us as we follow Jesus daily. In Psalm 149 verse 6 King David reminds us to let the high praises of God be continually in our mouths. This type of praise is not only a form of worship but spiritual warfare because while we praise God He is strengthening us and teaching us how to keep our focus on Him. One worship song I include in my daily prayer time is:

> ***I Worship You Almighty God*** there is none like you.
> I Worship you Oh Prince of Peace that is what I want to do.
> Is give you praise for you are my righteousness.
> I worship you Almighty God there is none like you.

Take time to meditate on the Lord while taking a sip of coffee. It is okay to be still and listen to the Lord. He desire to speak with you, whether it's through a scripture or a quiet still voice in your heart. Pause and close your eyes for a few moments and pray. Ask the Lord to give you a scripture or song in your heart at this time. He will quietly give you a word of encouragement or send someone to you with a word or song. Meditate on scripture. The Psalms is a wonderful place to start reading and meditating on at least one chapter a day. Let us make worship and meditating on the word of God a part of your daily habit.

There are many things we do everyday that are distractions from spending time with God – such as watching television, reading a book, calling a friend, mall shopping or going on the internet. One of the main ways the enemy deceives us is with distractions. If we are distracted by our situations and focusing on them then we are not focusing on the

Lord and worshipping Him. The enemy absolutely does not want us to worship God. He will distract us in a million ways. The enemy, Satan, would also have us believe that men and women in the Bible were so different back then and therefore worshipped God. The enemy also wants us to be self-sufficient, and to try to do things on our own. However, God reminds us that our sufficiency is in Him, (El Shaddai). In essence if we continue to focus on the circumstances in our lives then they become all encompassing and become our priority.

Worship is an act of surrender from our ways of doing things to God's way. A sacrifice of praise is a level of obedience that demonstrates offering yourself as a living sacrifice (Romans 12: 1 – 4). Whether in times of difficult or quiet times, or while waiting on the Lord for guidance and direction, that's the time to offer a sacrifice of praise unto the Lord. True worship is presenting your body as a living sacrifice, holy and acceptable unto God, which is your reasonable service. This type of praise and worship is not dependent on how we feel but on how we view God and for who He is. The Lord does not want us conformed to this world but transformed by the renewing of our minds.

The Lord restores our souls and renews our minds from old thoughts and we begin to realize how wonderful God really is. The restoration and renewal process goes on and on because we constantly want more of Him each day. Therefore, worship is not from our old ways and thoughts but through a renewed mind and spirit. I like verse one in Psalm 23 because the more we seek the Lord God through His son Jesus Christ in the power of the Holy Spirit, the more "we shall not want" anything else.

Our spirit is influenced by our attitude which affects how we worship. Our own worship is not sufficient. We must worship in spirit and in truth. It becomes our reasonable service each day whether at home, work, or in the community. Praise and worship in the spirit strengthens us in the inner man while we rest and wait patiently on the Lord (Psalm 37:7). During quiet or difficult times the enemy will use doubt and discouragement to try and keep us from trusting and worshipping God. Doubt and discouragement do not come from God. When experiencing these feelings immediately start praising and worshipping God. Praise and worship confuses the enemy. Worshipping the Lord when things are difficult or quiet, is an act of obedience and submission to the Lord because it is as if we are saying, Lord I don't fully understand what is going on but your ways are higher than my ways and you promised that all things will work together for good for those who love you and are called by your name.

CHAPTER SEVEN:

OVERFLOWING BLESSINGS OF GOD'S LOVE

Awake thou that sleep.... Walk circumspectly not as fools but as wise. Redeem the time for the days are evil

Ephesians 5: 14-17

The Awakening

August 2007 the Lord God impressed on my heart that this was the time of new beginnings. He was birthing something new in me, a new level and perspective. I have been waiting for months and several years. I feel like He has been saying to all believers, "awake thou that sleeps ... Christ shall give thee light" (Ephesians 5:14). While waiting continue

God In My Coffee

to pray in the spirit, praise Him in high praises, and seek His face daily through reading His word (getting to know Him). Not realizing it, He was using this time to prepare, train, and teach me how to "Learn of Me" (Matthew 11:37). For years, through trials and tribulation, I peaceably heard Him say "Wait on the Lord" (Isaiah 40:31).

Before a child is born there is a waiting period – which is a time of preparation for the new birth. Then there is a labor period – trials and tribulations – breaking down strongholds and the walls of Jericho in our lives. The Labor period is also a time of spiritual warfare between powers and principalities in the spiritual realm. Satan is trying to steal, kill, and destroy the promise that you have been given. But Jesus said, "I have come that you have life and have it more abundantly" (John 10:10). Satan wants to kill what is being birthed in you. But Jesus says, "be of good cheer because I have overcome the world." We are more than conquerors because of Jesus. He has already won the battle. God's Spirit lives within us therefore, greater is He that lives within us than He that is in the world. Hold on to what the Lord has promised and said He will do. One thing my husband and I often say is, when you're going through trials and tribulations it means you're right on track. Even Peter says that if you suffer for Christ sake you are blessed (I Peter 4:14). God's word is a constant reminder of His promises. One promise that has sustained me through many trials and has strengthened me is:

Scripture Promise: James 1: 12 & 17

Blessed is the man (or woman) that endures temptations (and trials) for when he is tried, he shall receive the crown of life; which the Lord has promised to them that love Him.

When He gives you a revelation regarding His word, write it down, search out the scriptures and seek the Lord daily, pray and praise. If He puts something on your heart to repent of, then repent and turn away from the wrong. Then, suddenly in God's timing, you will experience a breakthrough. Spiritual understanding causes a shift in the spirit realm – a Spiritual Paradigm Shift in the Heavenly Realm. When we have a paradigm shift we understand information from another perspective different from how we thought previously. The Lord gives us His viewpoint in a way that we have never foreseen. As we walk with God's Spirit of wisdom and understanding we experience and live the Word of God.

Let's Walk

Applying the Word of God comes from walking with His Holy Spirit in the new land that God has brought us to. He is doing it anew. God's Spirit gives us revelation knowledge, wisdom and understanding. He teaches us how to walk in this new understanding with God. But – not in our own strength. We can walk in newness of life, wisdom, love, and in truth because we are abiding and drawing very near to the

Holy Spirit. We are walking as one, in unity. Just as Our Father, Son and the Holy Spirit are one, so we come in agreement with the Holy Spirit. We abide in Him and He abides in us (John Chapters 14 and 15). We don't do anything without His leading and guiding. He is the pilot and we are in the passenger seat following His lead, walking in the path that He has already laid out for us. We are spiritually dead to our old way of doing things. Now, we wait upon the Lord (The Holy Spirit), who renews our strength. We mount up on His Mighty wings to a high place. He shows us things from His perspective. Then, with Him we run and do not grow weary and walk and do not faint (Isaiah 40:31).

As we walk with God through His Holy Spirit in this sweet closeness and fellowship He reveals secret things to us. He desires to reveal His secret things to those who revere (fear) the Lord. We reside with Him in His presence and His glorious light is revealed in us. The more time we spend with Him the more His light shines on us. He reveals His way through revelation knowledge and deep understanding of how to continue our walk with Him.

Scripture Promise: Proverbs 4:18; Ephesians 5: 8, 14

The path of the just is as a shining light, that shines more and more unto the perfect day.

For we were sometimes (in) darkness, but now we are light in the Lord; walk as children of light. Christ shall give thee light.

The Lord impressed on my heart in January 1, 2007 when I asked Him what was the theme and direction of my life in 2007 and He said: 1) Walk in the Power of the Holy Spirit; 2) Be not Afraid; 3) Tithe. I must be honest and say I understood His word but I did not know how to apply it. I kept seeking the word of God and meditating on scriptures that talked about "Walking". But all in all I pondered these words and waited on the Lord to give me understanding. Early one morning just before getting up I could hear the song "Holy, Holy, Holy Lord God Almighty" I woke up with this song in my spirit and very peacefully the Holy Spirit revealed the wisdom and understanding of the word "walk' which came from Him. We are simply to walk with the Holy Spirit, through life as He leads and guides. It's as if we willing submit to the Holy Spirit to lead as we dance.

In these perilous days we need the Holy Spirit's wisdom and understanding to get us through spiritual battles. Many darts and arrows will be hurled at the believer. But if we have a repentant heart and continue following the leading of the Holy Spirit, then the darts will be ineffective and nothing will come near us because we are covered under His wing and His truth is our shield and buckler. His truth humbles us and convicts us towards a heart of repentance. We are open to God's truth that reveals any area in which we need to confess and repent. Then He forgives, heals, delivers, and restores our soundness of mind. We must keep trusting and believing the Lord's wisdom and understanding for our daily faith walk. Just like Adam walked with God, the Lord desires that today

God In My Coffee

we walk with Him and His children in the cool of each day through His Holy Spirit.

Sometimes we forget the wonderful blessings and promises God has given us. I would like to list a few and challenge you to find more for yourself by reading the Bible and asking the Holy Spirit to enlighten your heart to see the blessings in the word of God.

As I list different verses please look them up for yourself so you can become familiar with reading and hearing the word of God and receive the blessings in the word for yourself. As you meditate on the word believe that the Holy Spirit will give you wisdom and understanding. When you start reading the word for yourself a great place to begin in the New Testament is the Book of Matthew and in the Old Testament the Book of Psalms and Proverbs. Continue growing in God's love. Everyday pray and seek the Lord by reading His word for about 10 to 15 minutes.

The Lord wants our love; heart, soul, and mind. He desires to spend time with us. Surrendering is our choice to turn from our old understanding, thoughts and ways of doing things. The Holy Spirit is our teacher and will teach us how to follow the Lord's way. If you let Him, the Holy Spirit will transform our heart so that we become very sensitive to His voice that we no longer want to do things our own way anymore (John 10:27). For example, as a wife, sometimes I act as though my husband needs my help when we are driving somewhere we've been the day before. When I get in the car my antenna goes up and I start navigating. This can be very irritating to

God In My Coffee

my mate. I think I am being helpful when in actuality I'm not trusting God or my husband.

The Lord God of Host delights to have us do His will and purpose and allow Him to fight the battle for us. In our own strength we are absolutely not equipped to fight the enemy. Zechariah 4:6 says, "not by might, not by power, but by my Spirit says the Lord." In our own confidence and willpower we can not fight the enemy, that is, spiritual warfare in the heavenly realm. In the majority of battles the enemy will try to control our minds. The moment we try to confidently do it ourselves, we are not trusting that God is able to handle the battle. We should deny our self-will and release our confidence to God – trusting and believing He will bring us through victoriously.

As the Lord transforms us by the renewing of our mind He also transforms our forms of worship. The more time we spend praying, praising, and worshipping the Lord the more we begin to realize how majestic and awesome God is. During these times He reveals a spiritual glimpse of His splendor and greatness. Praise and worship come in many forms.

A new form the Lord put on my heart was similar to a majestic chant. I heard a beautiful new sound as I was waking up early one morning. It was majestic and powerful with a musical high praise as if to prepare for the entrance of the King of Kings and Lord of Lords. I went downstairs to play it on the keyboard. It was short but it repeated several times majestically. My spirit felt like the Lord was reminding me to spiritually look at Him with awesome splendor, greatness, powerful and wondrous. Be still and worship Him in the beauty of His Holiness. While traveling on the plane back from St. Louis MO I was looking out the window and watching a beautiful red horizon sunset. I was just returning from a Joyce Meyer Women's Conference.

Each day look out the windows in your life and gaze into the heavens and see His glory and splendor. As we look out the window and sip our coffee, we experience a great rush of joy and gladness. He wants all of us to taste and see that He is good. Just look beyond yourself and your situation and let Him surround you with His presence as we focus on His Majesty and Excellence. I believe when God is showing us His splendor He reminds us that He is well pleased. It's like He is saying, "I'm glad you're taking the time to look at my glory. Keep looking and I will show you more." He has plenty for all of us to experience.

As you sit down sipping you coffee or tea and reading this book, pause and look out your window and allow Him to show off His glory to you right now. By faith, do you see Him? Keep looking, and you will find His presence. Almighty God desires that we seek Him first and His righteousness, *and then* all these other things shall be added (Matthew 6:33). This is a promise, we have a tendency to add the things before seeking God and then we find that we went the entire day without worshipping the Lord in the beauty of His Holiness. It is in daily prayer and meditation on the word of the Lord where we are equipped, prepared, and strengthened for each new day. Don't get distracted as we so often are. So,

God In My Coffee

stop right now and take the time to pray and worship the Lord God. I hope you find out what a wonderful honor it is to worship the Lord. I also hope you find out that worshipping the Lord changes from being a daily act of obedience to a time of relationship and fellowship where you can't live without Him.

Look at the Spiritual Growth worksheet at the end of chapter three and use it to write down your personal notes. Write down how you feel right now and what you think the Lord is trying to show you. You may be going through difficulties or trials. Write that down. When you write it down, the mystery is taken out of the situation and the enemy can't hold these over your head anymore. When you confess things that are in your heart and start praising God out loud it puts confusion in the enemy's camp. He gets mad and flees because he can not stay around when God is being worshipped. Write down what you think the Lord has been trying to teach or show you while you have been reading this chapter. Then write down what He has been revealing to you so that you can be triumphant from this time forward.

CHAPTER EIGHT:

A HEART OF THANKSGIVING

O give thanks unto the Lord of lords; His mercy endureth forever

Psalm 136:3

The more we recognize God's hand of forgiveness, lovingkindness, mercy and grace the more we want to thank Him for all He has brought us through. Trusting and acknowledging Him instead of leaning on our own understanding allow His wondrous love to be revealed in our everyday life.

Scripture promise: Proverbs 3: 5-6

Trust in the Lord with all of your heart
Lean not on your own understanding

God In My Coffee

> But in ALL your ways acknowledge Him and
> He will direct your path

Each day the Lord uses daily situations of life as opportunities to teach us how to keep our focus on Him and not on the things of this world. The awesomeness of this is, the more we spiritually focus and keep your mind stayed on Him the more we experience His peace, love, joy and strength through the trials of life. It does not mean we will stop having difficult circumstances. However, it means we realize God is with us, strengthening and bringing us through.

Scripture promise: Isaiah 26: 3-4

> Thou (The Lord) will keep him (her) in perfect peace,
> Whose mind is stayed on thee; because he trusted in thee
> Trust ye in the Lord forever:
> For in the Lord Jehovah is everlasting strength

Sometimes we forget to say thank you. But The Lord says in His word to have a heart of thanksgiving and rejoicing (Philippians 4: 4-6). So, let's take a few moments, while we sip our coffee and look out the window, to tell God thank you for all He has done, is doing, and will continue to do. One of the best ways to develop a thankful heart of gratitude is to read the Psalms and notice how often King David thanked

God – too numerous to count. Psalm 105 is a great chapter where David is expressing a heart of thanksgiving. Let's take a look.

Scripture Promise: Psalm 105: 1-5

> O give thanks unto the Lord; call upon His name
> Make know His deeds among the people
> Sing unto Him, sing praises unto Him, talk about all of His wondrous works'
> Glory in His Holy Name, let the heart of them rejoice that seek the Lord
> Seek the Lord and His strength; seek His face evermore
> Remember ALL of His marvelous works that He has done
> His wonders and the judgments of His mouth

Another common theme that David wrote about in the Psalms was:
Praise the Lord, give thanks unto the Lord
For He is good and His mercy endures forever
Notice in these psalms how David praises the Lord with a reverent gratitude. At the same time he also speaks of the psalms as a form of strategy and remembrance. He speaks these psalms to communicate with God. David believes no matter what is going on in his life. He trusts God to bring him through; therefore, He can praise God with a heart of thanksgiving and be grateful ever before He sees the

outcome of the circumstances. King David praises God before the battle is over, what faith! No wonder God called David a man after His own heart.

Abraham was another servant of God who was considered a friend of God. If you remember the story, he did not have a child until he was almost 100 years old. However, God promised him a son. Abraham believed God and did not doubt. When Abraham was 75 the Lord had promised him a son. He waited twenty-five years which means he waited to receive the promise. How many of us are still waiting on a promise? How many of us get impatient while waiting and almost miss the promise? Abraham not only believed God but he had a heart of thanksgiving. He was thankful that God gave him a son. Abraham was also thankful that he did not have to sacrifice his son because God provided a ram in the thicket. This was Abraham's greatest test of faith. He was victorious and experienced God as Jehovah Jireh, the Lord provides. I believe the more time we spend in the word, prayer, and meditate on the goodness of God the more we experience the same type of victorious living and be a friend of God. Remember we too will be tested to obey His commands and instructions that are provided in His word. He says in **John Chapter 15: 11-15** the following:

> These things I have spoken to you, that my joy might remain in you and that your joy may be full. This is my commandment, that you love one another, As I have loved you. Greater love has no man than this, that a man

lay down His life for His friends. You are my friends if you do whatsoever I command you. Henceforth I call you not servants: for the servant knows not what His Lord does. But I have called you friends: for all things that I have heard of my Father I have made known unto you.

As I read I Chronicles Chapter 16 and Psalm 105 the Lord impresses on my heart who He is and how to have a heart of thanksgiving and worship Him in spirit and in truth. In these verses are practical "how to's" and strategies of how we are to serve the Lord. Seven strategic guidelines are provided:

1. **Give Thanks**
2. **Sing unto the Lord**
3. **Tell of His wonderful acts**
4. **Glory in His holy name**
5. **Seek the Lord, seek His face**
6. **Remember His benefits**
7. **Worship the Lord in the Beauty of His Holiness**

CHAPTER NINE:

THE BLESSING

Blessed are the pure in heart: for they shall see God

Matthew 5:8

Hopefully throughout this book you have come to believe that your heavenly Father God loves you very much. He loves you so much that He gives gifts, offers promises, and provides instructions on how to follow Him through His Holy Word, the Bible. The Lord God sent His son, Jesus, to make a way for us to have eternal life and follow Him through prayer, worship, meditation on the word of God, and applying His word for our daily lives. The Holy Spirit teaches us how to follow Him so we can tell others about Jesus and eternal life.

Jesus promised that He was going away to prepare a place for us. He told us, "Let not your heart be troubled: you believe in God believe also in me. In my Father's house are many mansions." Jesus promised and said, "If I go and prepare a place for you, **I WILL COME AGAIN** and receive you unto myself: that where I am there you may be also." Then Jesus finalized the statement that answers our unspoken question by saying, "**I AM THE WAY, THE TRUTH, AND THE LIFE: NO MAN COMES TO THE FATHER, BUT BY ME**." (John 14: 1-6) Well, there it is in black and white, Jesus is coming back soon to receive His bride (us) to live with Him, forever. It is our choice to believe and receive Jesus into our heart. His Spirit is preparing us to meet our King of Kings and Lord of Lords.

My husband and I have a music ministry. We've had wonderful opportunities to sing for various types of Christian engagements. One of the songs we sing is called, "In All of His Glory." It's a beautiful song that glorifies God. As we begin the song my husband makes a very bold statement – "Jesus is coming again, the greatest epiphany of all times. But this time when He comes He's not coming as a little child but as King of kings and Lord of lords." Jesus will return as He promised. Are you ready? Is Jesus your Savior and Lord?

Remember what we said in the beginning still holds true. **Oh taste and see that the Lord is good.** The Lord God is sweeter than honey or cream. He is good to the last drop so allow God's Spirit to fill your cup until it overflows continually with His everlasting love. And finally, the Lord wants to bless us.

Let's read this together from Ephesians Chapter three verses 16 – 20:

> That He (God) would grant you, according to the riches of His glory, to be strengthened with might by His Spirit in the inner man. That Christ may dwell in your hearts by faith; that you being rooted and grounded in love may be able to comprehend with all saints what is the breadth, length, depth, and height. And to know the love of Christ, which passes knowledge, that you may be filled with all the fullness of God.
>
> Now unto Him that is able to do exceedingly abundantly above all we ask and think, according to His power that works within us.

How sweet our Father's abundant and ever flowing love is, such that He included the fullness of Himself through the Father, Son, and the Holy Spirit. We receive this rich blessing as we accept all of Him. The Lord desires to empower us with His love through His Spirit. He gives us deeper understanding through His word and He pours His rich abundant love on us so we can love others. He blesses us with more gifts and blessings.

My hope and desire for you is – that you believe and experience the overflow and fullness of God's presence everyday in your life as you seek Him daily. He will never run out of love for you and the secret is; the more abundant love you receive, the more you will desire, and the more you will give back to Him.

This makes God very happy because His senses your love for Him and in return He gives you more of Him. Wow, that's good stuff. The promises and blessings in the word of God prepare and strengthen us to do His plan and purpose for our lives. Receiving this abundant blessing fills you up to the point of overflow so that you can start your journey each new day as......

THE BEGINNING

CHAPTER TEN:

EPILOGUE

The Gift of Salvation

Salvation is another gift that the Lord offers to us. Because of the Lord God is great love and mercy He offers us salvation by grace. Salvation and grace are not earned or worked for because if we worked for it then we would boast and put a price on salvation. Boasting leads to pride and self-sufficiency. Since God created all things and gives us creative ideas then there is nothing we can say that we own because it all belongs to God. Therefore, the only thing we have to offer to Him is, ourselves. It is by grace we are saved, through faith – and this is not of ourselves, it is a gift of God – not by works, so that no one can boast (Ephesians 2:5-9). Maybe this is why Jesus said in the gospels, that it is easier for a camel to go through the eye of a needle than for some to believe and be saved. Salvation requires that

God In My Coffee

we let go of our pride and self-sufficiency in order to accept the free gift of eternal life by faith. There is nothing we bring to earn this gift.

Contrary to the world's belief, God longs to commune with us and wants us to get to know Him. The first way to get to know the Lord God is by accepting His son Jesus Christ as your Savior. Jesus is the way to eternal life. *Accepting Jesus* as our personal Lord and Savior means that we have been born again. However, if you don't know Jesus as your Savior, then pray the following sinners' prayer: "Jesus I have sinned, I repent of my sins right now and I confess with my mouth and believe in my heart that you are the Christ and the blood you shed for me on the cross cleanses away all my sins. Help me to experience and understand how to follow you as Lord of my life." After this prayer we believe you are saved.

Now that you have accepted Christ you still may not know how to walk and follow Jesus. For example, the distractions in life often lead us to doubt that we were really saved, question if God exists and whether we can *grow in Christ*. If we don't know who we are in Christ then we don't know how to be an overcomer and live a victorious life. But, through the Holy Spirit God enlightens us about His word.

We are God's children and as His child we have God's Spirit living in us. The Holy Spirit is our teacher and counselor. We learn more about the Lord God through reading His word. As we read, the Holy Spirit gives us understanding of how to apply what we are reading to our daily walk. While the bible is the blueprint on how to follow Jesus, the journey of a closer relationship with God also begins when we seek Him through prayer. As a child of God the Holy Spirit is the power source or activator that makes the Bible become alive and real in our lives. Faith is believing what God's word says is true, then acting on it.

SUGGESTIONS FOR FOLLOWING JESUS CHRIST TODAY

Here are a few more scriptures and words of encouragement to remind you of who God is, how much He loves you, and He will never leave or forsake us:

- Believe that the Lord really LOVES US
- Reach out and Receive His FREE Gift of Love (I John 5:16)
- Love the Lord God with ALL of your **heart**, soul, mind, and strength (Matthew 22:37)
- If you love me you will keep my commands (John 15:10)
- Seek the Lord First daily and all the other things shall be added (Matthew 6:33)
- **CHOOSE LIFE**: Choose Daily who you will serve (Deut 30:19; Joshua 24:15)

God In My Coffee

- Diligently seek Him. The Lord will reward those who do (Hebrews 11:6)
- Spend time with the Lord daily – Prayer, Read, and Meditate on the Word of God
- Submit yourself Daily-(Surrender)- Resist the devil and He will flee
- Guard your heart because out of it flows the issues of life (Proverb 4: 23-27)
- Keep your mind stayed on Him and the Lord will keep you in perfect peace (Isaiah 26:3)
- Come unto Him and He will give you rest for your souls (Matthew 11: 28-30)
- Trust the Lord and don't lean on your own understanding (Proverbs 3:5)
- Confess and repent daily as the Holy Spirit shows you your ashes
- Allow the Lord God to do a new thing in your life by: renewing your mind (Romans 12:1-2).
- Rejoice in the Lord Always, and again rejoice

WORDS OF ENCOURAGEMENT FOR DIFFICULT TIMES

- DWELL in the secret place of the Most High; abide under the shadow of the Almighty
- Fix your eyes on Jesus, who is the author and finisher of our faith (Hebrews 12:2)
- Fix your thoughts on Jesus (Hebrew 3:1)
- Stand and be strong in the Lord and the power of His might (Ephesians 6: 9)
- Pray and put on the spiritual armor of God daily: (Ephesians 6:10 – 18)
    o Helmet of Salvation (renewed mind day by day)
    o Breast Plate of Righteousness: Cover by Jesus' shed blood; we are in right standing because of Jesus Christ; He protects our heart with His Breastplate

- o Belt of Truth- The Spirit of Truth is our shield and buckler
- o Shod feet with the Gospel of Peace- as we walk and follow God
- o Shield of Faith – the quench those fiery darts
- o Sword of the Spirit- which is the Word of God

- Praying Always with all prayers and supplication
- Follow hard after the Lord God (Psalm 63:8)
- Let the High Praises of God continually be in your mouth and a two edged sword in you hand. (Psalm 149:6)
- Offer yourself to the Lord daily as a living sacrifice (Romans 12:1)
- Forgive yourself and others. Remember God is working ALL things out for your good (Romans 8:28)

REFERENCES

Bevere, John, 2005. Freedom from sin. (Video), www.messengerinternational.org

Herbert, Jeff. (2007). How to Worship. (Oral Presentation) Covenant Life Church, Springfield VA 22151 www.covenant-life-church.org

Institute for Creation Research (2007). Primary Love. www.icr.org.

Our Daily Bread. (2007) www.RBC.net

Stanley, Charles. (2007). In Touch Radio Broadcast Ministry. www.intouch.org

Wilkerson, David. (2001). Hallowed Be Thy Names: Knowing God as You've Never Known Him Before. David Wilkerson Publications Inc. NY, NY.

Printed in the United States
125925LV00004B/2/P